EVERYDAY LIFE IN THE HAREM

I am quite black and blue from pinching myself to be sure it really is me sitting here in an honest-to-goodness harem in the middle of Saudi Arabia. I guess it is.

I don't exactly know where to start this epistle, how to tell you about my life here which is so different, the family, my trip over. This total dependence on the male world is something you simply cannot relate to until you experience it. Although I thought I knew exactly what to expect, nothing could prepare me for the actuality of having absolutely no control over my actions.

For
Pat, Helen, and Emmett,
who insisted this be written.

For
Bob, who helped so enormously.

And for my daughter, without whom
this book would never have been
possible.
With Love.

EVERYDAY LIFE
IN THE HAREM

Babs Rule

A STAR BOOK
published by
the Paperback Division of
W. H. Allen & Co. PLC

A Star Book
Published in 1986
by the Paperback Division of
W. H. Allen & Co. PLC
44 Hill Street, London W1X 8LB

First published in Great Britain in 1983
by Blond & Briggs Limited

Printed and bound in Great Britain by
Anchor Brendon Ltd, Tiptree, Essex

ISBN 0 352 31758 2

San Diego, California
July 22, 1982

Blond & Briggs
Dataday House,
8 Alexandra Road
Wimbledon, London SW19 7JZ

Dear Mr. Blond,

I'm afraid I must admit that when my youngest daughter announced she intended to marry a boy from Saudi Arabia I was just about that far from delighted. The fact that he was a prince did little to improve my outlook on the matter. As far as I was concerned he traded horses and rode a camel.

They were married at the Islamic Mosque in Washington, D.C. I was there to throw rice with ill-concealed dismay. A few days later they left for Arabia.

My son-in-law is the oldest son of 'Prince Abduraman' and his first wife 'Princess Jewaher'. When my daughter gave birth to a son the following year he made them grandparents for the first time. He was my first grandchild also! This royal couple from another world and I shared a common bond; a bond which transcends culture and colour lines.

One day late in 1980 I was thrilled to receive a round-trip first-class ticket to Saudi Arabia from Princess Jewaher. Perhaps she was as curious about me as I was about her.

On June 24, 1981, I was off to visit a prince and princess who spoke not a word of English, to live in a harem, and to wear a veil.

It was a fabulous experience and my intended month stretched on week after week. I was half a world away by geography, ten thousand worlds away by life style. I learned so much about Arabian people and the role of women and young people that I simply had to share my impressions with everyone.

In order to protect the privacy of a family that was kind to me, I have used fictitious names and altered some of the facts, such as the number of sons and daughters in the family and their descriptions. The descriptions are actually composites of many people in Saudia today, and of the difficulties

5

exposure to the forbidden features of our culture are causing for them.

It is my hope that this book will enable young girls of European and English-speaking nations to understand better what they might expect if they marry into the Muslim culture, and that the rest of us may become more aware of the problems the Arabian Government faces as it joins the world powers, so that we all more clearly understand the drives, hopes and personalities of these people as they develop more and more of a voice in world politics and finance.

Happy reading,

Babs Rule

Saudi Arabia
July 5, 1981

Dear Pat,

At this point I am quite black and blue from pinching myself to be sure it really is me sitting here in an honest-to-goodness harem in the middle of Saudi Arabia. I guess it is.

I don't exactly know where to start this epistle, how to tell you about my life here which is so different, the family, my trip over. This total dependence on the male world is something you simply cannot relate to until you experience it. Although I thought from extensive reading, and talking with friends who'd been here, that I knew exactly what to expect, nothing could prepare me for the actuality of having absolutely no control over my own actions. At this point I don't know if this independent American career girl will make the adjustment or not.

Probably the best way to tell you all about it is to just start at the beginning and let it flow from there, so pour yourself a drink, old girl, and another one for me (Scotch here is $85 on the black market) and I'll get started.

You know how it was, when the invitation arrived, I was knee-deep in fiscal budgeting problems and personnel conflicts. I wasn't exactly meeting each day as a public school administrator with joyous anticipation. I was putting in my time. I told myself, 'No way, baby, you can't chuck it all and go traipsing half a world away.' Oh, couldn't I, though? I resigned my position, rented out my condominium, began packing my bags, and at the close of the school year I was on my way! All the mysteries of the East awaited me.

The first of these turned out to be the matter of a visa. One doesn't just pop in at the embassy and pick up a visa for Saudi Arabia! There are, to my knowledge, only two ways for a foreigner to get into the country. One is with a permanent work visa, issued *after* you have procured a position; the other, as in my case, is with a visitor's visa. These are available only through personal invitations and are issued by the minister of foreign affairs or someone. There is no such

7

thing as a tourist visa. Tourists are definitely *persona non grata* around here.

Arrangements were made for me to pick up my visa in London, before flying to Arabia. I was told I had been booked into the Dorchester Hotel in London and would be provided with a limousine. It turned out to be a Rolls Royce, powder blue inside and out and complete with a chauffeur in powder blue livery. I felt as coddled as a pregnant giant panda. However, if you picture me sweeping imperiously off the plane like the Queen of Sheba to my waiting limo, forget it! Whoever gave Mr. Pomfret (the family chauffeur) his orders had a thick Arab accent, and when they told him to pick up Prince Abdul Raman's mother-in-law, he assumed (rather naturally, I think) that he was looking for an Arabian lady. None got off the plane. They told him my name was B. Rule, but to him their Arabic accent made it sound like Beyrullah, so he had me paged as 'Princess Beyrullah.' I heard it, but you've got to admit it's rather a far cry from little old Mrs Rule of San Diego, California, so I ignored it. It took two and a half hours of standing around Heathrow before he arrived home, received my somewhat frantic phone call and returned for me. Thank goodness they had the foresight to give me his number. Would that they had been so farsighted for my connections in Arabia! But more on that later.

Mr. Pomfret was a charming gentleman of about 35. As we drove up to the very grand Dorchester Hotel near Hyde Park, the doormen swarmed around. I managed to walk into the lobby without tripping, slipping, or colliding – one part Babs Rule and one part imitation princessa!

My room was waiting for me; I loved it! The baths were huge and had fluffy white towels the size of a bedspread hung over heated towel racks . . . yummy! Too tired to tackle dinner, I drank the bottle of champagne I found in my room and went to bed.

Next morning I went down to breakfast and remembered a little sheepishly the last time I had tried to eat there. A couple of years ago my girlfriend Joan and I, dressed in somewhat scruffy jeans and pull-overs, had stormed the bastions of upper-crust London to stare at the famous and infamous. At both the Dorchester and the Ritz we were singularly unsuccessful in gaining entrance to their dining rooms. On this morning I ate my crumpets and jam with considerable satisfaction and drank an extra pot of tea for Joan.

The night before on our way from the airport Mr. Pomfret had asked me, 'Have you ever been in London before, Mum?'

I answered airily, 'Oh yes, several times,' and tried to look bored as we drove through that marvellous city I so adore.

'And where did you stay then, Mum?'

My God – I couldn't tell this elegant British chauffeur I'd stayed once at a 'Bed and Breakfast' and another time at the YWCA!

'With friends,' was all I could splutter, but that damnably chatty fellow wouldn't let it drop.

'Oh, and in what part of London do they live, Mum?'

My mind went blank – the only place I could think of was Kew Gardens. Oh, Pat, I sure hope that isn't the zoo! Wherever it is, it ended the conversation.

The next adventure was the visa. It took two days to procure it, but Mr. Pomfret had wired my hostess that it would take three. This was to prove a disastrous miscalculation.

I stayed at the hotel and lived it up, sailing into the dining room and ordering enormous meals of roast beef and Yorkshire pudding, wild strawberries and gateaux galore. All those marvellous English waiters hovering over me to pour tea, wine and water! I played the *grande dame* to the hilt, sweeping out with a casual 'put it on the bill please'. It ended all too soon.

Next came the flight to Saudia on British Airways. I think we swam over! Never had I taken a flight with so much liquor. Everyone was storing up for the long dry spell ahead. I couldn't keep up with the businessmen and returning Arabs, but I downed two Bloody Marys with hors d'oeuvres, white wine with the antipasto, and a couple of glasses of delicious red wine with the lamb. A glass of port went well with the dessert and I couldn't say no to a little Grand Marnier with some marvellous cheese and a rather spectacular pear. I believe I demurely declined an after-dinner drink, however, and remember that lost opportunity with a pang.

Suddenly we were approaching Arabia. From the air I could see the huge geysers of flame from the oil fields, beautiful against the purple of the night sky. When our plane touched down, the prelude was over; the show was about to start. I was not prepared for the opening act!

I had been told I would be met right at the plane door and taken to the V.I.P. lounge. There would be no bother with customs and other such inconveniences as are inflicted on the lowly masses. No one was there! I made my way from the plane to the pandemonium of the airport. It was fascinating – packed with humanity, dressed in the native costume of a hundred different nations. I picked up my luggage, found a porter and went through a cursory customs search. Once inside the main lobby the porter dumped my bags and held out his hand.

I looked around: every woman had mysteriously disappeared as quickly and silently as if the earth had opened and swallowed them all. There I stood, at 11:30 at night, a lone, unveiled woman in the Arab world with no Saudi money, no means to communicate, and no way to reach the family. Saudi families do not have home addresses, and they are not listed in phone books for the convenience of western tourists. They are very private people, as I was soon to be told. All I had was the Prince's name, and his business title. Later I was to learn how many princes there are with the same name. There just aren't enough Arabic names to go around! They are all named after each other. What to do?

At this point I offered the porter a handful of British and American coins, but he would have none of it. Keeping his hand shoved under my nose he kept saying something that sounded like 'fold money'. My smallest bill was $50.00. No way was I going to tip him with that! As I stood there pondering this dilemma, a hand reached out from behind me and gave the porter several sheets of 'fold money'. He trotted off while I turned to gaze up at an unmistakeably American face. Dempsey Deadderer, Texan, Aramco engineer, didn't have a halo and wings but he must have left 'em home. He clucked over my plight and waited with me for well over an hour, saying it was not wise for me to stand around alone. Then, as it became apparent that *no one* was meeting me we began wondering where I would spend the night. The message Mr. Pomfret was supposed to have sent as he put me on the plane obviously didn't get through. I was a day early. Mr. Deadderer explained that unescorted ladies could not check into a hotel in this country. The hotel management would get into serious trouble with the Arabian government if they were found catering to us. My situation did indeed look bleak! We decided to give the hotels a try anyway, and after a few disappointments, located one that would accommodate me in this emergency, but I was to register simply as B. Rule and *stay out of sight*. When the police checked their register I would appear as just another western businessman.

Dempsey drove me over, bag and baggage, to the hotel. What a fabulous edifice! Exotic and graceful, its black marble arches rose imperiously toward the lightening sky of pre-dawn Arabia. I checked into a beautiful room with huge sunken marble bath and an enormous bed. Three o'clock in the morning and I fell gratefully into a deep sleep. I was never to see my gallant rescuer again, but he will remain in my thoughts as one mighty fine Texas gent!

At nine o'clock I decided to brave the male world to find my family. While talking to the Indian and Chinese clerks behind the desk (who spoke fluent English), a tall and very distinguished-looking gentleman approached to ask if he could be of service. He looked like Stewart Granger, sounded like David Frost and introduced himself as the hotel manager. Upon hearing my problem he suggested I join him for breakfast (I couldn't go into the dining room unescorted) and then relax in my room, leaving everything to him. By now, of course, I was thoroughly enjoying the role of lady-in-distress, so off we went to breakfast and had a lovely chat. Glancing around, I was again aware that there was not another woman to be seen. The manager, Mr. Anderson, explained he would normally need to open a separate dining room for ladies wanting service. On the rare occasion that a family stays at

11

the hotel, the woman dines in her room. The idea of this arrangement made me all the more determined to linger over my meal. I had a lot of adjusting to do. After eating I did take the hint and return to my room, while Mr. Anderson began the search for Prince Abduraman. Periodically through the long morning he checked in to say they were having some difficulty, but not to worry. Heavens, I wasn't worried, I was having a ball! I never doubted for a minute that I would be found. Those hours in the airport last night had made me all too aware of how obviously I stood out in this Arab world. Word would get around as to where I was. They would find me eventually.

I was right. Around 2:30 in the afternoon Mr. Anderson rang to say, 'We have found them and someone will be here for you in twenty minutes. In fact I believe the prince himself is coming!'

'Wonderful! How did you locate them?'

'I pulled every wire in Riyahd, Dhahrain and Al Khobar and had all the police out searching. These princes like their privacy and they are very hard to find.'

'You are just marvellous,' I cooed as I hung up.

I was about to have my first lesson in Saudi time concepts! Excitedly, I gathered my things together, freshened my lipstick and prepared to see my daughter and grandson, and meet the family at last. Twenty minutes he had said. I looked at my watch. Only ten more to go! I waited, then I waited some more. Over three hours later I was summoned to the lobby. There stood my son-in-law, Prince Adbul Raman, with a red-check tablecloth on his head, and a flowing white robe! For some reason I hadn't expected him to be in native clothes. In his arms he held an adorable little one-year-old with enormous black eyes, and dark curly hair. My grandson! Beside him stood a heavily veiled figure. It darted forward and threw its arms around me. 'Mom!' it said.

'Good Lord, Lindy, is that *you*?'

Let me tell you, Pat, that is one shock of a lifetime to see your darling child done up in an outfit like that. I felt affronted and indignant that they would make my beautiful girl cover her face. 'Still,' I told myself quickly, 'this is one of the things to which I must adjust at once.'

Soon we were settled in a huge, black Rolls Royce, this time with deep red velvet interior – just one of the family's many cars, as I was subsequently to discover. I sat back for the trip through town to their home, happily holding my grandson, Tarek, in my lap, and chattering like a magpie of my recent adventures. I tried not to look at Lindy in her veils.

Looking out, I could see what appeared to be a city that had just undergone a blitz. Piles of rubble and construction everywhere; buildings partly torn down, others partly built. A city in a fever-pitch of progress. The traffic was terrifying. I closed my eyes and hung on, then squinted through them, not wanting to miss anything!

As we entered a residential district I was aware of nothing but high walls on all sides and tops of buildings peeking over them. We slowed down to around fifty miles an hour and headed straight for a large double gate. Again my eyes scrunched tight! But miraculously the gates parted and we rolled in to come to a halt in a wide circular drive.

We left the car and walked up an incline to a huge court-yard. It was now well past eight o'clock at night. The cement and marble courtyard was spread with six very large Arabian carpets upon which about twenty people were seated. Against a wall on a thicker carpet, surrounded by cushions, was a round little butterball of a lady in a low-cut dress, displaying the most impressive expanse of bosom and cleavage I have ever laid eyes on. 'Dolly Parton, eat your heart out,' I thought! This was my hostess, Princess Jewaher, Lindy's mother-in-law.

She smiled shyly, rose (an honour I failed to understand at the time) and kissed me on both cheeks. All the people who had been seated on the carpet then came in turn to kiss me once on each cheek and shake my hand. I was totally touched and disarmed by this show of loving friendship. What a warm welcome! I need not have been so impressed, for this is the ritual that takes place whenever two Arabs meet for the first time in the day, and the number of kisses you give or receive seems to indicate the degree of affection between the two of you at the time. I will never learn to anticipate how many are about to be planted on me – is this a two-kiss meeting, or a three-smacker? I always look somewhat like a turkey gobbler thrusting my head forward, back, then bobbing forward again, to receive each unexpected additional peck. This bobbing of mine is becoming a source of much laughter and good-natured mimicry as time goes by.

Well, Pat, there is so much more to tell you, but for now I must close as everyone will be stirring soon to begin a new day and I don't wish to miss a thing. I will write again in a day or two and tell you the rest of my impressions of my first days here in the harem.

Ma a Salaama (I think)

Babs

Dear Pat,

I meant to write several days ago, but things keep happening and I think I am getting lazier.

I want to tell you more about the night I arrived. As soon as we were settled cross-legged on the carpet (mmmmmm . . . was I truly sitting on a real Arabian carpet, under a real Arabian sky, surrounded by women in jewels and veils and young men in white *thopes*?) coffee was served. The tiny little cups were only half-filled, scarcely a swallow. What an art to pour a stream of hot coffee from those graceful long-spouted pots into a little cup less than a cubic inch in size which is held a good twelve to eighteen inches away! They pour with a swinging motion of their hand and somehow the stream of coffee unerringly hits that incredibly small receptacle without ever overflowing. I have not mastered it despite continual practice with cold water. Of course, none of the princesses can do it either. That is what servants are for.

My first reaction to the amber-coloured Arabic coffee was, 'Oh dear, its God-awful!' Thankfully, I soon developed a taste for the strange mixture of pale coffee, cardamon and saffron. They are wise to serve it in such small quantities; this way you aren't overwhelmed by it in the early stages. After drinking three cups you may decline a fourth by simply waggling the cup in a characteristic gesture to the servant who stands waiting to replenish it. This indicates to her without words that you are ready to switch to the syrupy sweet tea they serve in small glass cups. These two drinks are poured constantly all day or night, switching from tea back to coffee whenever a new guest arrives. The only task of several servants is to prepare these drinks and to stand there, pots at the ready, to keep refilling your cups.

Yesterday, totally bored with the endless sitting on the floor doing nothing but sip tea and coffee, I said to one of the daughters, 'How can you just sit here day after day and do nothing but drink tea and coffee, tea and coffee?' She looked at me incredulously. 'Why, I like tea and coffee,' she replied.

15

On the night of my arrival this went on for an hour or so, during which time I met Jewaher's six unmarried sons and three daughters, ranging in age from four to twenty-seven. I learned that no one spoke more than rudimentary first-year English and my host and hostess spoke not a word of it. I had mastered some fifty Arabic words with great difficulty. Communication was definitely going to be a problem.

It still is a major problem for my daughter, who has never been good at languages. She says that although everyone tells her she must learn Arabic no one helps her. She has asked repeatedly for a teacher, but none has been forthcoming. Of course, she has absorbed a little, and does her best to translate for us. Several other foreign brides have the same problem.

Soon it was time for my first experience with a Saudi meal. A large cloth was spread on the ground and servants appeared carrying huge trays about four feet in diameter on their heads. They were laden with food: roast chicken on beds of rice (with little black things I thought were prunes but which turned out to be cooked lemons); rice in tomato sauce; french fried potatoes; potatoes in tomato sauce; spaghetti in tomato sauce; spaghetti in lamb sauce; spaghetti in a sweet soupy mixture; eggplant in tomato sauce; *Jareesh* (Bulgar wheat and butter milk) with mutton; delicious crusty little turn-overs filled with spiced lamb called *sambusa*; dough balls soaked in honey; fresh fruit and pudding. With the exception of two or three dishes, the food was just like anything I might be served at home; only the over-abundance was different. We seldom serve three spaghetti, three potato and three rice dishes all at the same meal! I was disappointed; they weren't even exotically spiced.

This basic menu minus the *sambusa* and honey balls has been unimaginatively served every day so far with only occasional deletions or additions, usually in the form of the vegetable. In place of the eggplant we sometimes have green beans, squash or okra, almost always served in tomato sauce. Theirs is definitely not a figure-conscious diet.

We each had our own plate and with our right hand (the left is definitely taboo) scooped, tore, or broke off the food

16

from the main dishes. Oh, Pat! Have you ever eaten spaghetti with your fingers? What a mess I was, and *no* napkins! I slopped rice, squirted grease, dripped watermelon, dropped spaghetti, and in general slurped and spilled my way through the whole meal. My lap looked like the garbage can at a cooking school! *How* did they get food from their plates on the ground across the expanse of satin and silken garbed laps to their mouths? Not even the four-year-old had spilled a bite. I was a sitting disaster area! I looked at Lindy. She had apparently mastered this art very well and was doing beautifully. Everyone tactfully ignored me. Happily, I found it is considered extremely rude to look anywhere but at your own food while eating. The reason for this is that if you do look at someone, you may unconsciously give them the evil eye, causing the person to choke on their food.

I had been told that it is considered bad form to prop yourself with your arm or hand when sitting. The Arab women keep both hands gracefully lying in their laps, waiting to be waved in extragavant and lovely gestures as they talk. These infinitely fluid and continual gestures, many of them with specific meaning, help me considerably to understand what they say. At one hundred and eighteen pounds, my derrière does not have ample padding for prolonged floor sitting and I find it hard on both my fanny and my back not to prop myself up. Proud of my size eight rear in American levis, it definitely is not doing its job here. As the cement under these beautiful carpets becomes more and more noticeable, I squirm and shift miserably. As the days go by I am not adjusting to this and am also developing an extremely sore hip from sitting on the ground most of the day.

After the meal that night, my hands were thick with grease and sauce. I was shown to a nearby washroom with a row of lovely pink marble sinks where everyone washed, then our hands were perfumed by a waiting servant. The Arabian people are incredibly clean. Washing five times a day before prayer is required and that establishes a life-long tendency toward fastidiousness in all things.

Within a few days I was provided with a fork to make mealtime more pleasant for me, but they haltingly and politely explained that they thought this quite barbaric (though the young adults all enjoy using our utensils and I frequently find mine gone if I'm slow to arrive at meal-time). How can they possibly think a fork is barbaric? Well, who knows how well that fork has been washed, or who has eaten with it previously? Whereas, one knows exactly where one's hand has been and just how scrupulously it has been washed before and after dining. Imagine that? My first experience with another country's view of *our* cultural peccadillos.

After dinner Jewaher presented me with five beautiful lengths of material. At first I thought they were gifts to be brought back to America, but soon I learned I was expected to have a selection of suitable long dresses made as soon as possible. Jewaher retains three Pakistani tailors to sew for her household. They are very quick and can have your dress back the next day if told to do so by Jewaher or one of the young princesses. (If *I* tell them they take their time, I've discovered.) The way it works is that you draw a picture of what you want, or find one in a magazine. The tailor takes your measurements and the picture, then presto, the next day you have your dress, exactly as drawn. The only problem is, something is always wrong and the clothes never seem to fit me correctly. I have this silly American aversion to wearing a blouse that is cut too skimpily, a skirt that is too long, a dress with the seam up the inside of one arm and the outside of the other. Each time I cringe to see the lovely silks, brocades, satins and chiffons mutilated. I find that when I give them eight or nine yards of material to make a blouse, they will still cut it so small that I pop the buttons on my less than ample bust. All the material they can avoid using they keep for themselves and make up for sale on the market, or send to Pakistan. Although the workers are actually very skilled, they do poor work for the Arab women, who seem too naive to realise it. I would love to get my hands on some of this beautiful material to bring back to an American dressmaker.

Shortly before my arrival here the month-long celebration of Ramadan began. During this religious observance, everything is backwards and inside out. It is a time of fasting, when Muslims do not eat or drink from sunrise to sunset. According to their teachings they may eat and drink from sunset until they can tell a white thread from a black one by the light of the coming dawn. Then they must fast all day. This uncomfortable state is cleverly alleviated for many by simply reversing the activities of night and day. One gets up around three in the afternoon, dinner is served about three in the morning. Lindy has adjusted to *this* part of Arabic life all too well, I think!

Another adjustment that I had to make quickly was to the date orientation. Wednesday night is like our Friday night, because Thursday and Friday are their weekends and Saturday begins a new week. Confused? I certainly was.

About nine o'clock in the morning, my first night in Saudia ended, we all went to bed to sleep through the daylight hours.

It had been twenty-four hours since I had slept. I was trembling from exhaustion, but too keyed up to sleep well. Around five the next afternoon the servants brought me a tray of *sambusa*, vegetable soup, potato and beef, rice, sweet spaghetti, and beans in tomato sauce. Not my usual breakfast. I put away a large quantity of it and joined Jewaher outside for coffee and tea. Lindy and Abdul Raman were still asleep. She patted the rug, indicating that I was to sit beside her. Unable to talk to one another, we smiled, nodded, exclaimed and pointed. I watched as the servants and guests put in their first appearances of the day. Each bowed low before Jewaher, kissing her forehead and the hand she gracefully extended. The night I arrived was the only time I have seen her rise to greet any other woman. As I said, I had not fully appreciated the honour she did me.

I was now trying to sift out the jumble of people I had met the night before. The three daughters, Gada, Fatima, and Nura, were there, and five of her sons, Musab, Khalid, Saud, Hamud and little four-year-old Saad.

Suddenly I became aware that everyone else had scrambled to their feet and off the carpet. Glancing around I saw a tall, slim gentleman in white *thope* and *ghotra* (the traditional white robe and headdress of the Arab male) strolling across the courtyard. He seated himself on the other side of Jewaher, who had also risen, and all the family members went forward to give him the ceremonial kisses. I was then introduced to my host, Prince Abduraman. He was responsible for this huge household of three wives, twenty-three children, his own mother, and over a hundred servants with their families. I had not known what I expected but it was not this fine-looking, painfully shy, extremely devout gentleman. He rose graciously to greet me and clasped my hand in a firm, brief handshake.

On the night of my arrival he had been with one of his other wives, for he conscientiously rotated them in order every night, obeying the Koran's directive to treat each wife equally and avoid jealousy.

It is whispered that Jewaher is his favourite, however. She was a slender girl of thirteen when married to the fourteen-year-old Abduraman. She was his first wife and the mother of his first-born child, my son-in-law. The importance to Jewaher and Abduraman of their oldest son's wife and family accounts for my being here today, Pat.

More later,

Babs

My darling daughter Trish,

What a fascinating place this is! Remember how we adored Firenze in Italy? The feeling that we had been transported back to the days of the Renaissance? How I wish you could be here with me to see, hear and experience it all, to soak up this strange culture and meet these amazing people. In one situation they are as modern as you or I, then a capricious moment later they may be completely barbaric – superstitious and tribal. They are never unmannerly, however, and have a rare dignity that seems to remain with them even in anger. But they are also extremely hot-headed and emotional, so there is seldom much silence around here with so many people interacting all day long.

Their way of life revolves around the precepts set down in the Koran (their Bible). Not only their personal lives are ruled by the Koran, but it is also the basis for their entire governmental structure, which is religious rather than political and thus next to impossible to update. If you think we struggle with a plethora of antiquated statutes in America, think what the poor Saudi ruler is up against with a set of laws that are over 1,350 years old! Laws given to Mohammed, the Prophet, by Allah! You don't fool around with that sort of thing lightly!

Did you know that the name of their religion – Islam – means 'surrender' (to God) and that the name of the people who practise it – Muslims, Moslems, or Mohammedans – also means 'one who submits'?

Everyone has been eager to explain to me that Jesus Christ is one of the great prophets of Islam, as were Abraham, Moses, and others who came before Mohammed. But because neither Jew nor Christian followed their teachings, Allah sent another, Mohammed, the last of the prophets.

The Koran accuses the Jews of denying the truth, uttering a monstrous falsehood against Mary, and of crucifying Christ, also of practising usury, although expressly forbidden to do so, and of cheating others out of their possessions instead of giving alms. The Christians are even worse, for they deified Christ and devised the Trinity! According to Islam, Jesus was conceived in the womb of a virgin, but was no more than a prophet of Allah. 'Do not say "Three" ' says the Koran, for 'Allah is but one God.'

Because Mohammed brought us the final word from God, Islam is the one true religion in the eye of the faithful. Mohammed taught all that Allah told him and it was set down in the Koran and Hadith, the guides to Muslim life. The Koran is less than five hundred pages long and contains much that is in our own Bible. Everything they need to know about how to dress, eat, worship, govern themselves, marry, divorce, care for the old and the orphan, or treat their friends and relatives is to be found in these two books. They are to worship none but Allah, resign themselves to his will, and lead a good life through prayer, almsgiving, fasting, and making, if humanly possible, at least one religious pilgrimage to the holy city of Mecca.

I was interested as a non-Muslim to note that at the time of Allah's revelations to Mohammed, Mecca was the site of religious journeys already! It was a pagan city which worshipped (at a black stone called the Kaaba) not only Allah but three female deities regarded as the daughters of Allah. When Mohammed began preaching against idolatry he became very unpopular with his fellow townsmen, whose chief means of income was from the pilgrims. Not too surprisingly, they ran the fellow out of town. He dashed off to Medina and apparently stirred up a war between the two cities. At the cessation of hostilities a neat solution was reached in a treaty. Mecca was to accept the One True God with Mohammed as his prophet, but all the faithful would still be expected to make the pilgrimage to Mecca. The Kaaba is the centre of religious devotion for all Muslims to this day.

No one has tried to convert me. The language barrier is probably partly responsible, but I think it is mostly their innate sensitivity to my feelings as their guest. They would like Lindy to become a Muslim, I think but they do not proselytise or pressure her. The people who come to work here need not be Muslim, but they are expected to follow and respect the laws of Islam, such as no drinking, or gambling, and the women are expected to cover their arms and legs discreetly, despite the heat. The M'Tawas (priests) walk the streets with rods, and when they see someone improperly dressed or acting in a way contrary to Islamic laws, they are supposed to whip the miscreants if it is a minor offence, or cart them off to jail if it is not. I'm told they are not gentle with those rods either! Such is the power of numbers, however, that they are finding it increasingly difficult to chastise the many foreign women who, as workers or wives of workers, now walk the city streets in western clothing. Although it is rude and disrespectful to the host country, the 'ugly American' appears more and more openly in slacks and jeans. It is still rare in the religiously conservative capital of Riyadh, but is now accepted with a sigh of resignation in Al Khobar, and Jedda. A few of the braver, more wilful young Arabian women are now beginning to follow suit; another breakdown, or breakthrough, in their cultural pattern. Lindy tries not to embarrass the family, so she wears the required veils and gowns of a Saudi most of the time, giving in to the comfort of her American shorts and jeans only in the privacy of her own rooms.

Since alcoholic beverages are taboo, and the black market is horrendously expensive, home brew is very popular with the foreigners. A wide range of recipes exists and everyone exchanges them or cherishes them much as we do a new recipe for coffee cake, or Aunt Susie's kumquat pie. As even talking about it is offensive here, the nickname-loving westerners have invented a slang term for liquor called 'Sid Ekke' or 'my friend'. When Fatima walked into the room one day, proudly sporting her new American T-shirt, I burst out laughing. It read, 'I love Sid Ekke'. I explained that her shirt did not simply say 'I love my friend,' but translated into American humour meant 'I love liquor' – not exactly appropriate for daily harem wear by a devout Muslim girl. I have not seen said shirt since.

The government of the country is unusual. Fifty years ago, the last powerful tribe was defeated by Ibn Saud and his followers, who then united the land and named it Saudi

Arabia after the conqueror. At that time almost everyone was hungry, poverty was the way of life, and water was the precious gift of Allah, always in very short supply. Life in a tent is definitely not one of glamour in this vast desert wasteland.

Ibn Saud was himself very poor, but his generosity was legendary. Although harsh with wrongdoers, he was considered just and was deeply loved and venerated by his people. To this day, everyone sits spellbound whenever a tale is told about him, and when his picture is shown on television everyone stops to stare at it. They are sure to call my attention to it with great pride.

One of the pleasanter ways he thought of to unify the country was to marry the daughters or wives of the sheiks and princes he conquered. In all he took about three hundred wives! His last son, number forty-two, was born when Saud was sixty-seven years old and I'm told he was deeply saddened that he could do no more for his country. He raised his one hundred and nine known children in the ways of Islam, the traditions of the Koran, rejecting western ways. He also established the line to the throne in what might seem a somewhat short-sighted manner. It progresses from his oldest son, to the next oldest, and so on down the line of sons until there are none surviving. Then it apparently will be up for offers.

Some of his sons were educated in Great Britain or in America. They are westernised in their ability to understand us and to converse with us in perfect English. They bear us no love, however, and we need to take serious heed to the words of the Koran: 'Believers, take neither Jews nor Christians for your friends. They are friends with one another. Whoever of you seeks their friendship shall become one of their number.'

The first of Ibn Saud's sons to rule was apparently a somewhat profligate fellow who lived it up in high style and left the country in financial difficulties. In 1964 he was politely asked to step down, which he did, and his brother Faisal, who had been travelling all over the world since the age of twelve, trying to handle things first for his father, and then for his brother, became king.

I guess he just about saved the whole ball game. A quiet, unostentatious man, he managed quite successfully to balance necessary changes with the religious requirements of the country. But alas, you know how it goes with the good, they die young. Anyway, he met an untimely end, a victim of the Arabic custom which gives all men free access to their king. One of his nephews approached him with a pretended request and shot him at close range. That was in 1975.

Next in line was his brother Khalid, who is much loved by everyone I have been able to talk to, though admittedly that is a relatively small number of people. Khalid (or Kholid) still allows all his people (although men only) to come to him with their petitions. Each day he sees many of them; they go to pray with him and to eat with him. I have read in our press that Khalid is just a figurehead and that the highly westernised Prince Fahd actually runs the show from his position as Prime Minister. I tend to feel that he plays a major role in dealing with the western powers, but here at home the Saudis feel quite confident that Khalid is at the helm. Fahd is the Crown Prince, however, and next in line for the throne. After him comes Abdullah, commander of the national guard.

Each of the ministerial positions of government, and all of the higher positions within each ministry, is headed by a member of the royal family. It is the greatest example of nepotism extant in the world today. The Saudis do not look at themselves as a country in the same sense that we do, however. They consider themselves as one large family, the Sauds. They take pride in each other and share the responsibility, fostered by the Koran, that makes them seem such an enigma of socialisation and monarchy. The princes are maintained in the splendour of the proverbial oriental potentate, but they in turn set up free hospitals, a free phone service, free education, and a share of the oil royalties with every single Saudi citizen.

Honey, I know you have a million questions about your sister! Her letters home to us have never indicated the true state of her existence here. She has kept from us the despair and misery she has experienced in this strange and different world. I'm sure now that the reason the family sent for me was to try to make her happy. They are kind people and do everything they can to ease her situation, but they cannot change their way of life, and it is terrible for a free spirit like Lindy to live here. Unfortunately it tends to be the wilful, independent, headstrong type of girl who is willing to go against the counsel of friends and family to marry into an alien culture, and here they find that it is just those characteristics that make adjustment so impossible for them.

It is like being in a maximum security ward of a prison, except with velvet cushions and no English-speaking inmates. When she arrived she could not speak a word of Arabic and Abdul Raman deposited her here with his mother and promptly disappeared, which is the way with Arab men. Where he goes and what he is doing should not be the concern of his woman. He is often gone for weeks at a time, and she is here alone, unable to make her smallest wants understood, with nothing to do, and unable to leave the harem except to go visiting with her sisters-in-law. At least now she has the baby; before that it must have been unendurable. She doesn't complain, however, and is so pathetically happy to see Abdul Raman when he puts in an appearance I cannot believe she is the same independent girl we once knew.

The family seems to love her, and the girls and young boys try to copy everything she does. They are constantly in her rooms and so she has little privacy. She is closest to her maid, a darling girl from Thailand who is trying hard to learn English and seems to idolise both her and Tarek.

The family gives Lindy beautiful materials for clothes and lovely jewels. That is not enough, however, to compensate for one's freedom. It is terrible to expect a twenty-five-year-old American woman, used to an active, outdoor life, to sit quietly and drink tea and coffee all day long, spend her nights wondering where her husband is and what he is doing, and watch her life slip away. Although they shower her with gifts, they do not give her a telephone, a teacher, or a car and driver. Even the youngest members of their own family have their own cars and drivers. It is as if they want to keep her completely cut off from all that is outside the harem, unless strictly chaperoned. Now I, too, am a part of this prison-like life! But for me it is still fascinating and there is the knowledge that soon I shall be leaving it all behind, returning to the twentieth century once again.

I hope you received my last letter, and I also hope you *answered* it! Just a little 'hint' from Mom that I'm the teensiest little bit homesick and miss you very, very, much.

Love and hugs, darling,

Mom

Dear Maryanne,

I haven't heard a word from you, or anyone else for that matter! Have you all forgotten me so soon or is there something wrong with the Saudi 'male' delivery? The fact that there is no such thing as delivery to the homes here is very frustrating. Of course by having all mail sent to the male head of household, he is able to keep a close check on the correspondence of his wives and children, but it is very hard on the likes o' me. Surely the Prince isn't holding back my mail? Perish the thought, I guess it is just very, *very* slow.

I have been getting outside a little more. The young princesses, eager to show me their country, or using me as a fine excuse to escape the confines of the harem themselves, have been showing me around in a limited way. My first trip into town as a member of an Arab family was also my first experience with the veil! Although they were far too polite to insist that I wear one, I could tell they were very ill at ease about my appearance in public. Fair skinned as I am, and with this pale blonde hair of mine, I stand out even in America. Here I am as conspicuous as a mealy worm on the chocolate cake. To them a woman with her hair and face exposed is tantamount to an American woman strolling topless down Main Street. A double-take shocker!

My indication that I would be willing to wear the veil met with wide smiles of relief followed by much giggling and crowding around. Lindy, family and servants all sought at once to show me the proper way to wear the *elbaya*, an opaque black cape-like material which covers one from head to thigh, with a place to tuck your hands, as they must also be covered. Over this goes a doubled strip of black material called a *misffa*. It is rather like a piece of black cheesecloth of double thickness. They wrapped it around my head, covering my face from below the eyes to my neck. All this was topped with a lovely square of decorated black chiffon to cover my entire head. I could see through this, though not clearly, but looking in the mirror, I saw that my eyes were not discernible. I was

28

nothing more than a tall, slim, black blob. Under these layers I wore the full length dress of the Arab woman. Quite a costume for the 120° weather of Saudia in July. We all piled into the chauffeur-driven Mercedes belonging to Gada, the oldest daughter. Women are not allowed to go *anywhere* outside the wall unless accompanied by a man. I balked at this control but was told, 'You are much too precious to have to make your way alone. We see that you are always protected and cared for. No one will dare to bother or insult you.' I was only slightly mollified by this explanation. I've seen this type of 'care' lavished on horses in the States. I felt like a commodity, granted a commodity with some value.

We drove past many high walls, the tops of beautiful homes just titillatingly visible behind them, and came to the busy main thoroughfare of the city, someday soon to be one of the world's most beautiful communities when the rubble and machinery inevitable in new construction is finally cleared away. The wide, tree-lined boulevards already give evidence of it and the Arab love of cleanliness is apparent in their immaculate condition. They are swept down daily and the fine for littering is steep.

When we got out of the car and headed toward the shops I immediately realised an alarming problem. With all of us looking like refugees from a Hallowe'en party, tripping along in identical black costume, no hair or flesh showing, how was I to know who was who? I could just as easily wander off with some other little coven. I grabbed the edge of Gada's *elbaya*. She sensed my problem and laughingly pointed to the different bits of skirt fabric showing beneath our robes. This helped, but what if someone else wore a dress of the same material? I felt safer but kept a firm grip on her nonetheless. It was only a few days later that I did indeed lose everyone in the crowded gypsy quarters called the *souk*. I wandered around for almost half an hour before they finally found *me*.

Arabian women, even with their husbands, are not allowed to visit many public places, but this custom is gradually changing. Just a year or so ago the girls from good families were not seen in supermarkets. Now, accompanied by their drivers, some are enjoying this great diversion. I'm not sure if their parents are actually aware of this. However, I *am* sure their parents are not aware that some of them are even boldly setting up dates to meet boys there for brief and daring conversations, albeit heavily veiled.

Their supermarket is truly an experience: a glorified Fred Meyers, with pet stalls, jewellers, food, bakeries, florists, gifts and restaurants (for men only). Christian Dior shoes on racks selling for 200 riyals (about $65 American) was just one surprise.

A trip to the Euro Marche or to Safeway is like a trip to a meeting of the United Nations for it teems with foreign workers and their families. You will see tall turbaned Sikhs, beautiful sari-clad Indian women, delicate Taiwanese, Egyptians, Yemeni, Australians, Germans, French, British, Canadians, Chinese and many more gathering their week's supply of groceries and paying the outlandish prices unquestioningly. The supply of food is staggering, and one's eyes bulge with amazement at the delicacies from all over the world flown in to satisfy the culinary needs and desires of this myriad people. Never in America have I seen such a rich variety of fascinating foods. The only things missing are the alcoholic beverages and the meats of the pig . . . pork, bacon, ham. They do their best however. Ersatz bacon looks very real and when I saw the rows and rows of beer and wine bottled and labelled to look exactly like those brands found on the shelves of our supermarkets at home, they had a hard time convincing me that they did not indeed.contain alcohol. And would you believe it? When they drink this fruit juice (carbonated in the case of champagne) some of the Arabs actually think they are getting high and describe a giddy feeling they experience? Oh, the power of suggestion. Of course alcohol is easily bought on the black market for a high price, and drunkenness among young Arab males is a serious concern to the government and a deep heart-ache to the parents.

In addition to the supermarkets, the more adventurous Arab ladies are now able to visit the new boutiques that are opening up everywhere. I found it difficult to have a male salesperson showing me items of intimate apparel, but the women see nothing strange about this. The shops sell the top name designer fashions and prices are incredible, but you can't argue with the style! Although the Arab wives wear traditional garb exclusively at home, an increasing number of the younger ones buy western clothing for their trips abroad.

The *souk* is another place a few young women will visit. The *souk* (or *suq*) comprises blocks of open-air stalls selling every conceivable thing, much like Mexican markets except for the gold stalls. These simply must be seen to be appreciated. They are absolutely laden with gold. Row on row of belts, necklaces that look like huge bibs from neck to waist, and bracelets, all made of fine twenty-four carat gold, shimmer and shine as they hang suspended from the roofs of the stalls. The three walls of each stall are covered with earrings and chains, while showcases contain sets of precious stones, rubies, emeralds, sapphires and diamonds, set in gold and silver. The booths are crowded with people shopping and one wonders how long such a place could exist in the United States before an armed gang would graciously relieve everyone of their responsibilities.

This is where the Muslim treatment of thieves proves to be successful. If someone were caught stealing this gold they could indeed lose a hand. I had the opportunty to go to 'Chop Square' as it is called, where once a week the hands of the thieves are cut off. I believe it was the only sight I declined. They are warned about stealing twice but on the third offence, off comes the right hand and on the fourth off comes the other. It is pretty difficult to continue a life of crime with both hands cut off at the wrist. Also, unlike most other countries no one can give the excuse that their family was starving, as there is no real poverty unless it is caused by one's own wastefulness. This terribly strong act of justice does *not* deter minor theft, however. In fact theft is rampant. I would be robbed blind if I didn't keep everything under lock and key like the rest of the household. You see, the penalty is so extreme, that no good Arab will report someone for stealing unless it is very, very serious. They do not want to be responsible for the loss of another's hand.

One pleasant practice for the shopper is that of serving coffee and tea to the customer. Sitting and sipping a cup of coffee or a cold Pepsi while the salesperson brings you a selection to choose from is a relaxing, pleasant way to shop. *However*, I soon learned the need to plan a shopping trip with considerable more forethought than any Arab uses if you plan to enjoy this happy custom. On my first visit, as I was lifting my cup to take an initial sip, I was suddenly told, 'Hurry, hurry, it is time for pray.' Everyone jumped up and left the shop, blinds were drawn and the place was closed for half an hour. We sat in the heat of the car and waited. One of the many inexplicable habits of the Arabs which sets my teeth on edge is the fact that although they know everything shuts down five times every day for prayer, no one ever seems to know when to expect it or how to plan for it. The result is these constant 'hurry' trips to the hot car right in the midst of our shopping. I would mind the annoyance less if this was carried on through a serious devotion to religion, but almost no one bothers to pray. You will see an occasional old man spread out his prayer rug on the sidewalk and, facing Mecca, go through his ritual of prayer. But most people just stand around in idle groups or sit in their cars waiting for everything to open up again. For the businessmen in the offices, the salespeople in the shops, it has become the time for their coffee break. It is a custom which hinders the flow of business and fails to serve its purpose. But Saudia is a country run by religion and the Koran, not politics, and it is hard for us to understand that.

Although the shops are packed with people, very few are Arabian women, for the young ones who are forcing this new freedom are still in the minority. Most Arabian ladies are extremely shy, and are loath to go abroad, even when heavily veiled. The gypsy women who sell their goods in the *souks* are an exception. Princess Jewaher never goes out to a public place. Everything she purchases is brought to the house by the Bedouin (gypsy) who carries a huge variety of merchandise bundled up in enormous pieces of cloth. These big bundles are laid on the floor in front of her, untied, and out spill the treasures of the world; silk, incense, handcream, perfume, polyester, nailpolish, baby booties, men's socks, khol, spices, lipstick, lingerie, a myriad fascinating things. Everyone gathers around and selects what they want. Jewaher tosses gifts hither and yon to guests, servants, and anyone else she wants to favour. At the end the woman somehow comes up with a figure which Jewaher unquestioningly pays unless Gada is present. Gada at twenty-seven is still single and still going to school. The government, in its effort to educate the people, pays everyone to attend, and many of the young aristocracy such as Gada 'earn' extra pocket money by taking a course or two each term. Gada is not an average student, for at twenty-seven she still counts on her fingers to add seven plus four. Knowing this, it is a source of secret amusement to me to see her solemnly writing down the price of each item and then supposedly adding in her head these long columns of figures covering several pages, and composedly stating a figure close, but never identical, to that of the gypsy.

To Jewaher, who can neither read nor write, her daughter's talent must seem amazing. In actuality, Nura, the fourteen-year-old, is a far better student. It is only through Nura's daily improving English and Lindy's limited Arabic that I am able to communicate at all. Her grasp of mathematics, time and her country's history are superior to that of either of the other daughters.

Educational opportunities for women were started thirty years ago by the wife of King Faisal when she sponsored the first school. It was very poorly attended. Fathers were extremely hesitant to expose their daughters to learning, to allow them outside the harem. Gradually attendance improved as Faisal brought pressure to bear on the family heads. Many fathers who complied now regret their leniency. It has created much heartache for them as their girls went abroad and returned with demands for more freedom, the right to courtship before marriage, the right to careers outside the home. The schools are currently well attended, with government economic incentives encouraging even the lackadaisical students such as Gada. But the desires and needs of the government for an educated populace is at variance with the traditional role of womenfolk and is causing much friction. In talking with the fathers, one may speculate that the educational opportunities for their daughters could soon become quite restricted again.

Education for young men is also highly encouraged by the government. All expenses plus cash incentives are paid, and anyone wishing to study abroad is able to do so if they are at all capable. Again, the parental attitude toward school is not necessarily that of the government. I have been eagerly looking forward to the first day of school and the consequent absence for a few blessed hours of the six-year-old. The day came and went. After a couple of weeks I asked when the little darling would be going. Jewaher has decided he will not begin until he is at least ten, so that he will be old enough to 'hit the teacher if the teacher doesn't treat him well'. God help the teacher who is too hard on a prince.

This attitude fails to appreciate the government's dire need to develop professions and skills among its people. It is an extremely serious problem for a country where currently all skilled labour and management must be imported from abroad. This state of affairs leads to perpetual chaos. The Arabs themselves seem to have absolutely no ability to organise, and concern for time schedules simply is not in them. Coupled with this problem (you can imagine that foreign employees take full advantage of these eastern personality patterns) is that of language. Imagine trying to communicate orders when your workforce is comprised of labourers from fifteen or twenty different countries! They pay for their own lack of technical know-how by having shoddy workmanship palmed off on them continually. The exquisitely polite Saudi will seldom object strongly. As a result of this, everything looks satisfactory at first glance, but upon closer observation is a disaster.

One young man we visited had contracted a Pakistani cabinet-maker to build a set of cabinets for a kitchen of his new home. Of course, the man appeared about a week late to begin with, but he then proceeded to build an excellent set of cabinets. At first glance one couldn't ask for better work, but stepping up to them I saw a long rip in the formica on the counter. I would not have accepted it, but the young man dolefully explained that he had paid in advance and that the cabinet-maker had done the job well; it was no one's fault that the material he used was faulty. They also purchased a shining new set of appliances; huge refrigerator-freezer, which, had all the gadgets worked, would have done everything but can your peaches; a washer; drier; dish washer; and cooker. Nothing worked! The oven door kept falling off; the Corningwear top was misaligned, so you had to hunt for the place to put a pot; the washing machine skipped a cycle; the drier overheated and scorched the clothes; the refrigerator wouldn't stop making ice cubes! I swear I've seen a movie like that somewhere!

The quality of almost all American merchandise there is so inferior that I was humiliated to acknowledge it as American. Fine name brands that I have used successfully for many years in my own home all seem to be defective when purchased by a Saudi. Do our companies deliberately palm off their duds on these people? Or is it possible that they are all counterfeit?

Arabs absolutely adore anything electrical. The men are truly overgrown six-year-olds in this regard . . . if it moves, buy it. They cannot resist a new coffee-maker, juicer, video tape, cassette player, or electronic game. My daughter constantly moans over the amount of unnecessary gadgets and mechanical toys her husband carts home. Invariably when it arrives he finds that all the parts are not in the box, or that some are defective. It is their own 'Ensh Allah' (God's will) approach to everything that makes them ripe for this sort of rip-off but I don't like to think we actually take advantage of it.

The plumbing and electrical work here is a disaster. In most homes where I have had a chance to observe, it appears that they do not plan for these until the house is completed. Possibly this is because both services are relatively new luxuries in their world. One would think, however, that once aware of their existence they would be able to adapt their construction methods to accommodate them. As it is, the home is built with the finest of materials: gleaming ceramic tile work from floor to ceiling proliferates in every bathroom and the huge kitchens; marble is much in evidence in floors, stairways and countertops; exquisitely carved woods are utilised for doors and panelling. The homes are simply sumptuous, *but* take a visit to the powder room and glance around while sitting there! You will find that the ceramic tiling invariably has a chunk the size of a basketball taken out of it wherever pipes must come through. It is then filled in crudely and ineffectively with plaster. Kitchens are mutilated in the same way.

I have the lovliest of bedrooms, with deep rose carpeting on the floor in the finest wool plush and rose velvet drapes at the window. My bed is enormous and the scalloped headboard is quilted in the same lavender and dusty-pink silk as the bedspread. The two lamps on my bedside tables have shades made of the same delicate material. But all this decoration is marred by an unsightly patch on the wall. I decided to move the bed to cover it, so I fabricated an excuse about better lighting and rearranged the furniture, only to discover that the hole for the electrical outlet *behind* the bed was far larger and uglier than the one I had planned to hide. Back went the bed to its original position!

That exercise, by the way, is the only physical exertion I've had so far in this place! I'm sure I shall be an absolute mess by the time I want to get back into my fitted skirts and pants again. The life of the women here is such a sedentary one. The lack of activity coupled with the extremely starchy diet leads pretty quickly to obesity and heart trouble, which in turn makes any exertion difficult. The young girls have the most incredible figures and fluid walks, but not for long. Everyone is interested in my appearance and they ask many pointed questions: 'What do you eat? What medicine do you take? What cream do you use on your face? Are you wearing a bra?' Probably the main reason for this constant curiosity is that in this land of roly-poly pouter pigeons my size eight figure must appear positively emaciated. I tried to explain in my usual mixture of sign language, Arabic and pigeon-English that I don't do anything special, but that American women are all very active, cleaning, working, running after children, dancing, maybe playing a sport, swimming and walking. The Arab lady sits or reclines all day, every day, all her life. No wonder that by mid-thirties their figures are gone, by mid-forties the skin tone is shot, by mid-fifties they begin to shrivel and by mid-sixties they are old, old crones. Looking in the mirror I could honestly, and most happily, admit to looking fifteen years younger than most of my counterparts. Now *that* is a very nice feeling! Even if it is not that I look so young, but rather, that they look so old. But how will I stay this way if I, too, am waited on hand and foot, get no physical exercise other than my own poorly-disciplined sit-ups, and continue to swallow all this fattening food in my usual 'last meal' approach? I'm sure it will soon be goodbye size eight, hello size twenty. I simply must be more regimented about my daily sit-ups, and as you know I hate the thought!

Lindy, once so very energetic and active with skiing, swimming, riding, running, tennis and dancing, has succumbed to this sedentary life and does very little of a physical nature now, apart from sporadic romps with the children. Once in a while she tries to interest the other girls in exercising, and she has taught them many games, even hide-and-go-seek. Nervous tension must keep her thin, however, for she is really very frail and wan-looking. This life simply is not conducive to robust health and it subtly robs you of your desire for any exertion.

I'm hungry for news of home, so when you write, if you have the time, I'd really appreciate a little update on the local and national scene both politically and economically. I wouldn't know if *Portland* is still on the map! I'm sure some mail will be getting through to me soon!

Best ever,

Babs

Dear Aunt Helen,

You know, there are some similarities between La Jolla and Arabia. They both have abundant sunshine, palm trees, and wealthy people. There, I think, the comparison ends.

Can you imagine a world where no one ever plays bridge, or mah-jong, golf or tennis? Where the girls can't meet at the yacht club for lunch and there is no cocktail hour? Can you imagine having to take a man along when hitting the sales at Neiman Marcus? And can you picture yourself spending all day making yourself beautiful for a man and then he doesn't take you out?

Jewaher has three daughters who have grown up in this atmosphere. Their personalities are interesting.

Gada, the second child of the union, feels her responsibilities as the oldest remaining at home. She is very regal in her bearing and often imperious in her attitude. Because of this I find her by far the least endearing of the family. She is an exemplary daughter, however, dutiful and respectful to her parents, loving and generous to the rest of the family. Although she has been 'abroad' numerous times, she is loyal to her country. She recognises its drawbacks, but says, 'This is my country and these are our ways, I would not wish to live anywhere else.'

Gada has the most spectacular figure I have ever seen. How does a waist that small support a bust that large. And her hips – the Italian who first said 'Mama mia' must have been looking at someone with Gada's measurements. Her walk is very slow and she seems to glide along, her skirts swaying most provocatively. I was quite disenchanted to discover she has very flat feet, which hurt, and that accounts for the slow, stately walk. She steps carefully, ve-e-e-r-y carefully!

One of Gada's most annoying characteristics, as far as I am concerned, is her method of treating everyone as her personal handmaiden. She is polite, but simply orders you to do things instead of asking, and always assumes you will do it! When she liked several of the blouses that Lindy had brought from the States, she simply sent her maid down to get them. She had decided to have the tailor make copies. It never occurred to her to inquire if Lindy planned to wear them during the next few days. Lindy was glad to be able to contribute something, but her pleasure might have been greater had Gada thought to ask her if she might have them first.

Another time we were out and her hair was bothering her. She held out her hand to me.

'Give me your bobby pin.'

No 'please', no 'May I borrow?' Just the imperiously outstretched hand. On that occasion she did not get it.

'I'm sorry Gada, it's the only one I have,' was my answer.

Gada looked mildly startled, murmured a noncommital, 'Oh,' and tucked her hair behind her ear.

Her maid is never far away, but once in a while she will say to me in a peremptory manner: 'Hand me the phone,' or 'Pick up my hanky.' I take a perverse pleasure in merely calling her maid when she does this. Her favourite command, which I have found no way to avoid is, 'Give me your pencil.' The maid doesn't have a pencil.

Gada has had several proposals of marriage because she is known to be a fine young woman from a good branch of the family, but she has turned them all down. Since she is soon to be twenty-eight I wondered about this and have been told that she is deeply and despairingly in love with a cousin who is committed to his monogamous marriage. She suffers greatly, but, with the regal bearing of the princess she is, gives no sign of it whenever she sees them together, which unfortunately is frequently. This tragic, unrequited love and the quiet dignity with which she bears it, makes it easier for me to accept her somewhat overbearing, arrogant manner.

Oh, I almost forgot, twice a year she gives all of that season's clothes to the servants in order to make room in her huge wardrobes for the new ones. I was in her room with her sisters and several servants when she was weeding everything out. She selected thirty-seven of her favourite things, and tossing them to me, said, 'Take to your maid in America.'

My maid in America! I couldn't wait to get back to my room and start trying them on. Alas, nothing came even near to fitting. You can't put a 40–22–40 item on a beanpole.

Gada's sister, Fatima, is totally different; warm, generous, funny, and wild, she is also sometimes rude and sulky. She had seen enough of the outside world through video-taped American films, and heard enough from her friends and brother to think it was the life she wanted. She was miserable, how would she ever bear the quiet, safe life of the harem year after year? She wanted boys, dancing, dates – everything that was denied her. One heart-aching night she slit her wrists in an agony of despair. Once having done so, she had the sense to realise she didn't want to die and summoned help.

Poor Jewaher and Abduraman were beside themselves; what could they do with this unhappy, wayward teenager? They decided to allow her to accompany her aunt to London for a few months. It cheered Fatima immensely and she had a wonderful time, but if they had expected her to return and assume the role of the obedient Arabian daughter, they were wrong. She returned more westernised than ever. She tries not to upset them, so her rebellion takes the form of deceit. She chain-smokes behind locked doors, and sneaks out to places that, as the daughter of a good Muslim family, are forbidden to her.

A bowling alley has recently opened which is reserved for women two nights a week. For the most part the women are foreigners – nurses, secretaries, teachers who work for Aramco and other large companies, and the wives of the company men. A few young Arabian girls have dared to steal in from time to time and Fatima is one of them. She is fully veiled and in the company of her driver. This may seem almost ludicrous from our point of view, but if her parents knew what she is doing they would feel much as an American mother or father does when their beloved daughter joins a hippy commune.

The way in which young people have gone about making contact in this highly segregated society is enterprising, and makes use of two modern conveniences, the automobile and the telephone. Each night you will see dozens of cars tearing up and down the main street of the city. One set of cars will contain a cluster of young girls, all fittingly veiled and decorous; the other cars carry a crowd of gay young blades out to catch the hidden eyes of the girls. They race up and down, peering in at each other as they pass, slow down and pass again. When the girls see someone they consider attractive they roll down their windows and shriek at their drivers to stop in a most 'undecorous' way! Then the boys, all prepared for this development, toss slips of papers into the open windows. On the papers are their names and phone numbers. The girls then go home and initiate the call. They could never receive a call themselves from a boy, but there is no law in the Koran that says they may not telephone him first. A time is set to meet at the Safeway or Euro Marche, and a romantic adventure begins. Such is the courting game here in the land of Islam.

All the young people do not engage in these shenanigans, of course, just as, although a law was passed in 1980 which allows a young man to see the face of his intended, some do not avail themselves of the privilege. They say the mystery, allure and excitement would go out of their marriage were they to know ahead of time what their bride looks like. On the other hand, some go to extravagant lengths to get a glimpse of a girl. I heard of one wily fellow who rented the home next to the maiden he was interested in, and sat there with binoculars, waiting for her to go for her daily swim in the pool.

Because virginity is so essential, girls are almost paranoid about accidentally rupturing the hymen. They do not ride horseback for this reason, and what with their fear of magic, evil eyes and *jinn*, they are always terrified that someone will hex them or something will happen to make them 'become a woman', as they phrase it. Several times when I was showing them various exercises they were afraid to try them for this reason, though how in the world they thought deep knee bends could be dangerous escapes me.

The youngest daughter is a delight. Charming and affectionate, Nura is not only the most intelligent of the girls, but also the most beautiful. Her figure is fabulous, and unlike her

41

older sisters her size thirty-eight bust is still firm enough not to need strong wires and engineering wizardry to keep it where it belongs. She has adorable dimples and an enchanting smile she uses to devastating effect.

Nura is caught between her sister's rebellion and the strict Muslim attitudes of her parents. She has taken up smoking with her sister and inhales deeply one cigarette after another. She wants very much to see the world, but fears she will never be allowed to leave the harem until she marries, because her father has decreed his daughters will not be subjected to western cultures again. This causes her much unhappiness although she would never dare to approach her father with the thought that she is discriminated against as the only child who has not had the opportunity to travel. How all this will end I don't know. Prince Abduraman hides from the questions, interests and concerns of his multitudinous family by retreating behind his newspaper whenever he is in their presence. Communication with him is very difficult. Whenever they feel they simply must discuss something with him it takes several days of mustering up their courage and bolstering each other before they do so. Puzzling. Exactly why this is so, I don't know for I have never seen him anything but gentle, kind and calm in their presence. Still, he gives an answer and his word is law, so perhaps they hate to broach a subject because once they have and he has rendered a decision contrary to the one they hope for, they have no more options. Unlike American youngsters, the girls do not whine, pester or throw tantrums.

Although Nura has moments of sadness over what she thinks may be a bleak future, her feelings are not those of American teenagers who argue with their parents that 'all the other kids get to do it'. In Nura's case very few of the other girls have any more freedom than she does; in fact most of them have less, for Jewaher and Abduraman are lenient parents. She is greatly influenced by Fatima and by the American films they watch, but she also has the strong tradition of the family and many of her friends to counteract the influence. To an American it is surprising how many of the young girls do *not* wish to be liberated. They feel safe, loved, cherished, protected, and have no wish to exchange that feeling of loving security for the right to do their own 'thing', to 'go it alone' as it were, to experience the 'freedom and independence' I hold so dear. They find our way cold and lonely, even frightening.

As I contemplate this strange phenomenon it occurs to me that there are women just like this in the States, women who are born, grow up, live and die in the same small town. They have no need and no desire to explore beyond it. I wonder at their lack of adventure and curiosity, but who is to say which way of life is the richer.

As for Nura, at fourteen she is the irrepressible, boisterous, fun-loving child one moment, the dignified, seductive-looking woman the next. She loves a no-holds-barred wrestling match with her fifteen-year-old brother, when, skirts a-fly, she bites, pinches, kicks and gouges with laughing, squealing intensity. Two minutes later she sits decorously veiled and coyly feminine in the presence of her father or a visiting relative.

Nura is also a born mimic and keeps everyone doubled with laughter as she unerringly picks the recognisable characteristic of each of us and then mimics it to perfection. As she walks, talks or gestures, we shout out the names of her victims with the gleeful knowledge that we are right, so accurate is her portrayal. Her favourite impersonation of yours truly is to bob back and forth for the kiss on the cheek, finishing with a helpless shrug and a giggle.

Though I do not wish to upset their life-style or influence them in any way, I fear that my presence is a strong pull toward westernisation, for she is obviously fond of me and tends to copy me more than any of the others. This, coupled with Fatima's behaviour, may combine to sway her away from the ways of the Muslim.

I can't help but worry about this half-girl, half-woman who has so much delightful *joie de vivre* at present and may be heading in another year or two for inner turmoil, confusion, sadness, and even tragedy. Such are the problems facing everyone in Saudia today. I'm banking on the strength of their family ties and religious faith to see them through these difficult times of adjustment. If we have any hope of surviving the problems facing our teenagers with our splintered, fractured family life, then they should pull through also.

One of the strange manifestations of this segregated life which young people are forced to live is homosexuality. I say 'strange' because I have not yet figured out how important a role it plays in their later lives. I have not met many mature men who display any evidence of it. They are all married, and seem very happy with their wife or wives as the case may be, and with the many children they sire. The young men, on the other hand, seem to be blatantly involved in homosexual affairs.

Since there are no heterosexual social activities, young men spend their time of adolescent curiosity almost entirely in the company of other young men. I'm told that there is little incest because of the Koran's insistence on the virginity of Islamic women at the time of marriage. The retribution against any poor girl who goes to her marriage bed otherwise is certainly a deterrent to incestuous activity. But there is no such restraint upon the young men and boys.

The first practice that seems strange to a westerner is the holding of hands and kissing that goes on among Arab males. Please understand me, this is not indicative of homosexual leanings, it is simply a cultural difference that is worthy of mention because of the contrast with our masculine handshake. Once you adjust to it, it seems very warm, natural and charming; just one more example of their affectionate, open manner. On the other hand, during their adolescent period this hand-holding takes on extreme characteristics. You will see two boys walking along, arms entwined, or hands clasped and when one must drop his hand for some reason it is not unusual to see him reach out with the other so that body contact is not lost, like lovers loath to let go for even a moment.

Prince Musab has a 'friend' of whom he is more than passingly fond. He spends all his time on the phone to him when not in his company. He is forever in debt to everyone in the family because of the many extremely expensive gifts with which he showers his friend. He has pictures of him everywhere in his room, and wears a necklace engraved with his friend's name. Seldom have I seen such open and constant displays of love amongst the high school students in America.

Now my quandary is that I don't actually know whether Musab is a true homosexual, or if this is the phase that any normal young boy would go through when deprived of a female object of his adolescent yearnings. The rest of the family laugh at him much as some of us do when encountering an acute case of 'puppy love'. Jewaher seems to be noncommittal, at least in my presence.

As for me, perhaps I have at last met a 'Fairy Prince!'

Much love always,

Babs

Dear Bill,

Although I have been writing letters like mad to all my friends and even to casual acquaintances, to say nothing of my daughter and relatives, I have not received a single letter in return. What can be happening to my mail? I know someone must have written by now. It is getting very lonesome here with no word at all from the outside world. Talk about feeling cut off!

You wouldn't believe the place I am living in. This home of the Prince's is more like a medieval village than a home. It covers an area about the size of two city blocks surrounded by a high wall. Within this wall are several separate little communities. Each wife has her own area comprising her own home, the houses of unwed sons over the age of ten, those of the unwed daughters, the guest houses for married sons or daughters and their families (where I stay), the kitchens, laundries, garages, gatehouses, as well as the quarters for unmarried servants and separate homes for the married ones. In addition, all these facilities are repeated for the Prince's mother, and dominating all is the somewhat larger, more elegant house of the Prince himself. Slavery was abolished a few years ago and though many of the servants born into slavery chose to stay on, they are now paid each month. Other servants are hired on two-year contracts from Egypt, Yemen, Pakistan, Thailand, and the Philippines. Their life is good. Monthly salaries are very high by the standards of their own countries and are completely free of tax. Many of them send every cent home to be saved for the day when they return to set up successful businesses of their own in their native lands. All their expenses are paid, including all personal items, clothing and health care. Transportation is paid for a month's vacation in their homeland after eleven months of work, and of course, all transportation at the beginning and end of their contract. They receive expensive clothes and often many other gifts, as the family would lose face if their servants were not well dressed. Favourites receive gifts of twenty-four carat gold jewelry and the like. Those who were once slaves and now spend their lives devoted to their families are so well provided with beautiful jewelry and fine clothing that they are sometimes impossible to tell from the family except by their demeanour and the role they play.

No one works too hard. There are so many to share the load. There is a personal servant for each member of the family; guards, chauffeurs, cooks, launderers, sweepers, cleaners, tailors and an assortment of house servants who simply pour tea and coffee, run errands and so on. Favourites are allowed the privilege of eating with the family. I made myself immediately popular with most of the servants because, unable to tell who was an honoured guest and who was the servant, I treated them all the same, kissing and hugging indiscriminately. Except when Jewaher is having one of her rather frequent temper tantrums their life is very, very pleasant as life in Arabia goes. Any one want to sign up? Rudimentary Arabic is requested.

Lindy's and Abdul Raman's house is just like a well-appointed guest house in the States. They have a large bedroom, modern bath, perfume room (honestly! A *room* just to hold all the many bottles of perfume on a long, marble-topped dressing table), a small kitchen, dining room, and living room. When her son married, Jewaher had the entire place redecorated, with western chairs and couches, bedroom and dining room furniture. The kitchen and bath were entirely modernised with the latest equipment. Television, stereo and video tape provide an entertainment corner in the living room. All is in excellent taste with quiet, monochromatic colours in beige, white and brown. She worked very hard to make it as attractive and as much like home for her new American daughter as she could. Lindy was deeply touched. Jewaher is very sweet, and before I came she would often sit for long hours with Lindy when Lindy wept with homesickness and loneliness. She couldn't express her sympathy and understanding in English, but her loving manner and eloquent eyes brought what little comfort was to be had, and Lindy is very fond of her.

All Saudi homes are not like this one. Prince Abduraman

is quiet and unpretentious. He cares little for worldly things, leaving it to his wives to uphold the family position as best they can. Elsewhere these feudal estates are being torn down and huge homes resembling quality hotels consolidate everything under one roof. These buildings still divide the quarters of men and women, however.

Even in the modern homes of men educated in America and married to American women, *purdah* (seclusion of the women) is observed whenever the husband has guests. The wife must remain in her own quarters until the guest has departed. This banishment is a practice that causes much irritation and resentment among the western wives I met, but is one they have no choice but to obey. An Arab will almost never introduce a visitor to his womenfolk, and of course they are never invited into the harem. That is why my visit is so different. I *am* one of the womenfolk!

Another custom deeply resented by these young wives is the role played by their mothers-in-law in bringing up their children. The position of the mother is more powerful than that of the wife, who is expected to conform to her Arabian child-rearing practices, no matter how wrong or bizarre they may seem. It is hard to stand by and watch your little son taught to slap a servant, see him allowed to spit or kick, and watch them feed him a box of chocolates just before his dinner. But if this is hard, it is terrifying to see traditional superstition take precedence over modern medical practice when the child is ill. These circumstances create a power struggle between the mother and the young wife which the wife always loses, for the Arab man will side with his mother. He is bound by religion and tradition to obey the ruling of his parents as long as they are alive and mentally sound. The desires of the individual are always secondary to the happiness of the family unit for a good Muslim.

The methods of child-rearing among the royal family amaze me. As an educator you can imagine I have a hard time keeping my thoughts to myself! But Arabs do love babies and small children. It really is a delight to see a gruff man's eyes light up with unfeigned pleasure when a little toddler enters the room. The youngest are smothered with love, as all the members of these huge households, family, friends and servants alike, carry, kiss, hug and play with them constantly. That part is great. I've always felt you can't give enough love, but these royal children are allowed all licence and are never punished for misbehaviour. Young princelings are trained to be arrogant, demanding, and totally self-centred, above the law and subject only to their king, the Koran and their parents.

One day Hamud, the six-year-old, stood idly in the middle of the sitting room tearing chunks off a loaf of *pita* bread he took from a freshly baked pile that had been brought in on a large silver tray. He would take a loaf, tear the chunks off one at a time and toss them over his shoulder to the floor. A servant on her knees behind him quietly picked them up as they fell. The family sat idly watching. After seven or eight loaves had been senselessly demolished he tired of this game, and turning grabbed the servants arm, sinking his teeth into it as hard as he could. Grimacing in pain, she stood there, silently enduring until he stopped. She could not raise her hand to a prince, and his family saw nothing inappropriate in his behaviour.

Little princes are seldom chastised unless they do something to upset their mother. I have often seen them spit in the faces of the servants, who simply turn their head and wipe away the spittle. Biting, kicking and slapping the servants and the children of servants is common. Princess Jewaher trains them to slap at about the age of one. She makes a servant bend over on all fours, holds the hand of the little one in hers and repeatedly hits the woman on the back. As they grow older the children learn that this behaviour is not necessary, but their place is clearly delineated in their minds forever more.

Seventeen-year-old Musab is a polite, effusively friendly, charming young man, but his imperious attitude toward those who work for him is insufferable in my eyes. One day we went to the market, and the one servant who accompanied us was soon laden with the purchases of the three girls and two boys. She also held the hand of the youngest and carried a diaper bag. Musab sauntered out of a store with a small bag of candy which he handed to her. She tucked it under her chin. The ludicrousness of this laden woman and the strapping young man strolling, empty-handed, suddenly got to me. I snatched the bag of candy and shoved it back at Musab. 'I think you can manage this one yourself if you struggle a little,' I said. He couldn't understand my words but the meaning was clear. His eyes widened, he looked startled, but he took the bag.

Another day we all sat on the lawn outside my quarters. There were swings and lawn chairs, and although Arabian women are not comfortable in chairs for very long, they enjoy an hour or two in this pleasant, park-like setting when the weather is cool enough. One of the very elderly ex-slaves sat in a chair to my left regaling us with stories of olden days. Musab approached us from the rear and walked to the chair on which the servant sat. Seeing him, she quickly jumped out of it and squatted on the ground just as he gracefully lowered himself into it. It was obvious he expected the chair to be empty by the time he reached it. I couldn't help wondering if he would simply have sat *on* her had she failed to scuttle out of the way fast enough!

On another occasion his fifteen-year-old brother Saud arrived when all the chairs were taken. Without bothering to look at her he casually snapped his fingers at a servant woman who appeared to be seventy. She ran for a chair and, lifting it high over the heads of the seated group, placed it in front of him. No one offered to help her, though she was old and frail and they were all young and healthy. I gritted my teeth and refrained from assisting her myself with some difficulty.

The prevailing attitude was brought home to me resoundingly at the home of Prince Saleh, an American-educated man married to a woman from Cedar Falls. We were discussing the marital break-up of another couple of similar backgrounds. The family did not want the wife to take her two young sons back to America with her. I could think of many reasons why not, but the one given by Saleh astonished me.

'The problem', explained Prince Saleh, 'is that if the children are educated in America they will not learn how to talk down to their servants.'

'Well, actually, that isn't the most important value they must learn,' I smiled.

'Oh yes, it is for a Saudi Prince!' he replied gravely. I decided it was time to change the topic of conversation; that remark was a stopper.

Perhaps you can begin to imagine the difficulties our diplomats face in dealing with the Saudis, who are so unperturbably and implacably sure of their own importance and inviolability. Used to instant obedience and having every whim gratified since birth, they have a sense of *noblesse oblige* toward the servants and gypsies (non-royal Arabs) but consider them definitely inferior to themselves.

Do write when you have time, I'm sure some mail will get through to me soon.

Fondly,

Babs

Dear Maryanne,

Still no word from home! I'm still worrying about my waistline and plan to get started on those push-ups any day now.

One thing that amazes me here is that with all this sitting around the women don't indulge in many activities of a sedentary nature either. I never see sewing, embroidery, or knitting. No one paints or sculpts, and of course, no one reads. No one in our household plays cards or games. I mean it is *Dullsville* around here if you think about it. My daughter had brought them a game of Chinese chequers and they would play this for hours until they lost all the marbles. I understand the men are quite good at chess, and they have a card game, which they explained condescendingly that they couldn't teach me because women are not mentally able to learn it! (Ah, love those Arab men!)

One game the women of all ages thoroughly enjoy is to shuffle across the carpet to create static electricity, then they try to touch you unawares. When the shock causes you to jump or squeal, everyone dissolves into puddles of helpless laughter. The servants are a source of entertainment for them as well. Zeneb is very good at telling fortunes, and several of them dance. An old ex-slave tells fabulous stories into which she weaves the names of her listeners, keeping everyone on the alert. She is an excellent mimic and even though I understand little of what she says, I enjoy her.

One day as we sat drinking our tea and staring idly into space, the story-teller suddenly leapt to her feet and began a mad leaping and whirling. She jumped, twirling high in the air, bent her body low in a wild side-to-side sweeping motion, then leapt again to whirl madly around the room. Aghast, I watched the feverish motions of this old woman, the incredible agility with which she swooped, swayed and leapt, the length of time that she continued exhausted me. I tore my eyes from her whirling body to look at the others. Their faces showed no particular expression, almost an indifference, much the same as when Hamud had torn all the bread into little pieces.

'What is the matter with her?' I gasped.

'She has the *jinn*,' explained Nura, matter of factly.

At last she collapsed exhausted in a heap on the floor. She appeared to be unconscious. Jewaher waved her hand and a servant left the room to return with a brazier containing a potent *oudh*, or incense. She passed it over the old woman and under her nose, much as we would do with smelling salts. Slowly the woman rose and, glancing neither right nor left, returned to her original seat and took up her tea as if nothing happened.

I was wide-eyed. They had told me that *jinn* can enter the body at any time through any of its orifices, some *jinn* are playful; some are very evil. I have been carefully warned that when I use the toilet I should be particularly careful to keep my mouth shut, for *jinn* frequently come up from the nether world through the toilet and will enter the mouth of anyone careless enough to have it open at the time. Now they've got me telling myself, 'Just remember to keep the lid down when brushing your teeth, old girl!'

Even the educated women are superstitious in a shame-faced way. A few years of schooling cannot erase the beliefs of a people quickly. The Koran acknowledges the existence of *jinn*. Some people are thought to possess the evil-eye and one must be careful not to offend them. It is necessary to be careful in looking directly at someone, for if anything unpleasant should befall them you might well be accused of having caused it. The belief that the hex is frequently put on marriages, business affairs and social events is a tidy way of escaping all responsibility for any disaster or unpleasantness that might transpire. 'I didn't do anything, there was a hex on it,' always meets with understanding nods of the head.

Well, the next time things go wrong at work you might try telling the boss it wasn't your fault, there must have been a hex on it. After all, there must be something good coming out of this place besides oil. Maybe we've been missing a bet!

Cheers,

Babs

August 3, 1981
At home in Saudi
Arabia

Dearest Trish,

It seems as though I have been here in Arabia a lot more than some weeks when I think about how long it has been since I've seen you. Life is very quiet but also full of interest. An interesting mixture, no? I'm always amazed at the way in which they conduct their lives; they are truly an incredible enigma, these nomads turned sophisticates. How anything is ever accomplished I'm sure I don't know. We are always rushing to go somewhere we never get to, dressing for guests who never arrive, waiting for important papers that never show up, and in general changing our minds a dozen times a day. How they ever make up their minds to procreate and then remember to follow through must be a major achievement. On the other hand, from the number of children each wife produces around here, I guess they have that part down pat. I am learning to submerge my American expectations of efficiency and expedience and accept their casual, if not relaxed, approach. I'd love to see *you*, my independent, intelligent, career girl, in this world of male supremacy.

It is certainly nice to be waited on like this, though. I just leave my clothes on the floor (remember how I would scold *you* for that?) and they are picked up, washed, ironed and in my closet that night. There is nothing to do here, but you can do it any time you want to. If you miss a meal you simply tell the cooks and in a short time a freshly prepared feast will appear wherever you happen to be. Everyone seems to sleep when they feel like it, which takes some getting used to. People saunter in and out at different times.

Two days ago it was El Eid, the ending of Ramadan, and rather like our Christmas. The streets are hung with strings of lights and the men have a constant round of dancing, parties and festivals to end the month of fasting.

The women all have a huge feast and run around visiting to show off their newest clothes. I was told that by tradition we must not sleep for thirty-six hours, staying up all night, all the next day and night until midnight. They explained that there would be many, many visitors and I must wear my finest clothes and jewels. Everyone had their hair done, their hands and feet were decorated elaborately with designs of henna; and Gada had five new dresses to wear throughout the celebrations.

Although we hadn't gone to bed until 5:00 a.m. with all this anticipated excitement, we were all up and dressed by 9 o'clock that morning. We assembled in the 'best' sitting room to drink our tea and coffee and meet the first of the guests. A bevy of black blobs arrived with an assortment of overdressed children almost immediately. Shortly afterwards we piled into the car and drove around the corner to the entrance of the grandmother's house. It was my first visit to any of the homes in the compound other than those of Jewaher's family. Her house is so attractive: the sitting room is large and cool, with an exquisite and enormous oriental carpet of pale beige flowers cut in pale, pale pink, blues and turquoise. There is a large marble and gilt table in the centre of the room, and beige velvet chairs are lined up like a beige guard of honour around the periphery of the carpet. Velvet drapes of the same soft beige complete the decor.

Beyond was another lovely room decorated in the traditional Arabic style of thick carpets and cushions, with no other furnishings but the cabinets for the tea and coffee pots, and the tiled sunken area for the heating of the coffee urns.

We returned home for a large dinner and then each went to change and prepare for the evening visits. My eyes burned and I felt very tired, but I bathed and dressed in a silk gown of pale green with delicate sprigs of flowers all over it. Lindy loaned me her emerald necklace, bracelet and ring. Heavy and over-done in my eyes, I would have felt more comfortable in my little pearl choker, but then, what do I know about elegance? Lindy said it would be expected that she loan me something they would think appropriate. Ready once again, we entered the sitting room ... deserted. We wandered around all the other sitting rooms and favourite places. Not a soul. We returned to Lindy's room and sat waiting to be summoned. It was a long wait. Hour after hour crept by, we were tired, we were hungry. Finally we found a servant and asked where everyone had gone without us. Nowhere! They had all gone to bed! Arriving guests were simply sent away, I suppose.

So that's how it goes; after all that fuss and preparation! No apology, no explanation when they finally began drifting out, just, 'I fell asleep.' Now they felt great while we were a couple of zombies. We headed for a much-delayed sleep ourselves with a good deal of grumbling, I assure you.

As the routine re-established itself after that fiasco, one day seems to blend into another. Go to bed late, rise late, join everyone in the 'Beige Room', greet the visitors who come daily to sit with us, at half past one each day repair to the 'eating room' where the huge midday meal is spread on the floor for anyone present. At the conclusion of the meal Jewaher rises and goes to her own house for a rest. About four she reappears to sit on the swing in the grassy little park in front of my house. Here guests join us, along with many small children, and the servants bring the tea and coffee on huge trays. Often at this time of day mint is added to the tea for a refreshing change.

Darkness comes very quickly in the East. I am never prepared for the sudden transition from daylight to dusk, but with it comes the beautiful sound of the muezzins calling the faithful to prayer. As the last 'Allah' rings out and lingers in a long, drawn-out call, the sky turns from pink, through rose to deep purple and then to navy blue. As prayers are completed Jewaher rises from her prayer rug and makes her way to the upper courtyard where the carpets have been spread for us. Here we spend the early evening hours beneath the stars and moon of the soft Arab sky. We drink more coffee and tea, exchange a few desultory words, watch the outdoor television and sometimes have an evening snack. After a couple of hours Jewaher again rises and migrates, this time to the 'Green Room', where we continue the sipping of coffee and tea. By now all the family is with her; unmarried princelings, three daughters, the three small boys. The closeness of a Saudi family unit is always very apparent at this time of day. Only one or two close friends will still be with us, and a few servants. If it is Jewaher's night with her husband she will depart very shortly to finish the preparations she has carried out through much of the day. By the time he arrives she will be as beautiful as is humanly possible, bathed, shampooed, perfumed and oiled, carefully made up and gowned, fingers and toes manicured, body hairfree and sleek. She will await him with an eager anticipation I find it hard to sympathise with, considering the fact that he keeps her locked up in there for his convenience, while he can, if he wishes, cavort all over town.

Strangely, I am finding that I am not as bored with the quiet, dullness of the routine as I was in the early days. Somehow each day has something that is a little new and different to intrigue me, and I find to my amazement that the little things of life here take on significance and interest far beyond what they would if I were at home. In the States I led such a busy life! I believe I called it 'productive', remember? Up at six each morning to shower and dress for work, then off to the office. Rushing from one meeting to another, conducting the business of the school, into the classroom, evaluate a teacher, write my reports, answer my mail, solve a student crisis, check the fire alarm, meet with the custodian, check on the cooks, a hundred little details. Four o'clock meant more meetings with parents or salesmen, often a quick hamburger before a board meeting, PTA meeting, budget meeting, administrative meeting or one of a dozen committee meetings. Weekends brought shopping, housework, gardening, socialising, entertaining, maybe a visit from you, perhaps one of the frequent conventions out of town. A hectic pace that never ended. Switching from that life to the indolent existence of the harem took a little adjusting, but I must say, I took to being waited on with total joy, never a backward glance at the old New England work ethic. I find I savour the incidents of each new day with a fresh appreciation. I will suffer another form of culture shock when I re-enter the real world.

Jewaher runs her household from her position on the floor. Servants bring her a huge metal basin and trays of spices wrapped in cloth. She dumps several pounds of this, a cup

58

of that, a tablespoon or two of another, and so on, mixing and blending until it suits her, then it is taken away to the kitchen to be used by the cooks. She carefully selects the *oudh* to be burned at each occasion. *Oudh* is very important part of Arabian life. They love the smell of incense, but it is also a status symbol, for it is incredibly highly priced. Inexpensive varieties are only for the gypsies. People who can afford to do so pay fantastic prices. One day Jewaher bought a kilo each of two different kinds and the bill was 20,000 riyals, or about $7,000 American. The price *can* reach as high as $150,000, they tell me!

Another task Jewaher seems to enjoy is that of picking over the baskets of fresh fruit and vegetables brought in daily for her approval before being purchased by the servants. I am crazy about the taste of the delicious Arabian dates, tree-ripened and huge. I know I shall hunger for them when I return home. I have learned too, to eat them while they're still turning from yellow to orange; hard and crunchy, they are very good and very different. There is one fruit, hard, small, somewhat pear-like in appearance, whose name I don't know. I have never seen it before in any of my travels and after tasting it I can see why . . . yuk!

Food is always an interesting adventure, but I have been waiting somewhat apprehensively for the day when I will be offered the eye-ball of the sheep. Traditionally this famous Arabian delicacy is offered to honoured guests. Here I am just family and it seems to make its way into the women's quarters only for very special celebrations. A study in mixed emotions! I certainly don't want to eat the thing, but I resent not having the opportunity. There is that good old male priority again. I am beginning to develop a definite dislike for the opposite sex! Too bad, I've always found them rather charming up to now.

One thing I have eaten of course, is camel meat. My introduction to it was not, to my mind, the greatest. A large soup tureen was brought in and laid before Jewaher, who stuck her hand in, felt around and pulled out a huge foot! Yanking off a too large chunk she handed it to me. Obviously it was considered choice by the rest of the group and they watched enviously as I took a tentative bite. Red, stringy, with gelatinous pads and a degree of gristle, I found it didn't taste particularly strong, but it wasn't difficult to deprive myself of a second portion.

One night the problem of what to do with an apple core came up when we were seated on the carpets in the courtyard. There were no plates, napkins, or receptacles. I watched Jewaher through lowered lashes . . . as she took her last bite she casually tossed the core over her shoulder and one of the servants promptly picked it up. Shades of Henry VIII! Delighted, I followed suit. I've always wanted to do that!

Having servants constantly available has led to some pretty crude manners. At least I assume that is what led to them. Perhaps it is rather that in a tent in the desert table manners are not necessary. Or, in this case would you call them 'floor manners', since they do not eat at tables? One of the snacks of the Arabs dearly love is seeds; pumpkin seeds, water-melon seeds, sunflower seeds, any kind of seeds. They buy them in huge plastic sacks and everyone sits around eating the seed and spitting the husk onto the floor. Each evening the entire floor is covered with them, giving the room the appearance of a huge bird cage badly need of cleaning. I find this habit one of their less attractive, but every morning the floor is immaculate again.

I guess I should mention that just like the folks at home we send out from time to time for pizza and Chinese food. It's funny to see the regal Gada munching on a slice of pepperoni pizza from a cardboard pizza box.

Commercial candy is a comparatively new addition to their lives, along with Pepsi. Now I can just hear you saying, 'Here goes Mom on her usual "junk food" soap box,' but really, in the past the Arabs have had beautiful teeth, startlingly white and strong. This will undoubtedly change for they lack the dietary knowledge to realise the harm that great quantities of junk food will have on their children's general health. From the cases and cases I see being loaded into the cars by the chauffeurs at the supermarket I would say, 'Hock the jewels and buy Pepsi stock.'

Responsibility for the lives of so many servants consumes

a portion of Jewaher's time each day, for there are dozens of squabbles, petty thefts, and various domestic problems to be dealt with. One day a fist fight broke out in the kitchens between two of the cooks. Jewaher called for something which turned out to be a stick about an inch thick and three feet long. She marched in and began flailing away, right and left, the blows landing on the poor fellows with a resounding whack! I was amazed at her strength for I had never seen her move before except to roll from one sitting place to another. She wielded the rod with fury and although the fight stopped almost immediately, they each received quite a few bruising blows before she was through. This was followed by a tongue lashing equally strong and delivered at the top of her voice. You have never heard shrieking until you have heard an Arab woman yell. When it was over she stamped away, dripping with perspiration, but I couldn't get over the feeling that she had secretly enjoyed every minute of it. As a means of venting frustrations with your life, it sure beats hell out of smashing your best china cup against the wall!

The other day I entered the sitting room only to jump back immediately. The screams and shrieks from Jewaher were the worst I had yet heard. I felt the nausea from sudden tension well up in my stomach. *What* could be happening? She was so angry the house seemed to shake with it. Servants stood in silent clusters, eavesdropping outside the doors. They looked at me round-eyed. I joined the group and strained unashamedly, I'm afraid, to understand the Arabic words Jewaher hurled in a frenzy at some poor culprit. Suddenly the doors flew open; I saw the servants Zeneb and her husband Mohamet standing rigidly before Jewaher. Zeneb had her arm in a sling, her face was bruised, her head and jaw bandaged. Yosseph, who is Jewaher's male link with the outside world, left the room. He returned shortly with several men and some papers. Jewaher asked a few questions, some at the top of her voice, then, turning to Zeneb, she asked if she was willing to be divorced from Mohamet. Zeneb indicated that she was more than willing. Next Jewaher asked Mohamet if he wished to divorce Zeneb. 'You bet!' Jewaher's next words were the equivalent of 'Get on with it then.' Mohamet said, 'I divorce thee, I divorce thee, I divorce thee.' Whereupon they were told by Yosseph to put their marks on the paper. It was witnessed by the marks of the other men present and that was it . . . divorce Arab style. Simple, cheap and quick. Too quick, in this case, for a week later Zeneb was crying, sobbing and begging to be reunited with her beloved Mohamet. But poor old Mohamet had to turn his passport over to Yosseph at the time of the divorce, and with amazing speed in comparison to everything else around here, an exit visa was issued for him to return to Egypt the next day, *sans* jobs, *sans* wife and *sans* the right to work in Saudia again.

Later that day Lindy and I learned from Yosseph, who speaks a little English, all that happened. The night before, Zeneb and Mohamet had an argument. He accused her of unfaithfulness with half the male servants in the harem (and no, the male servants are not eunuchs). She grabbed a can of insecticide and sprayed him in the eyes. He grabbed her earring and ripped it out of her pierced ear. She began hitting. He broke her wrist. As I said, Jewaher has many 'little domestic problems' to deal with. In spite of what would seem at first to be a very quiet life, she has extremely high blood pressure.

Not all the problems have such unhappy endings. Bedur, another one of the house servants, was pregnant, very much so, and finally the day arrived. Bedur scurried to her quarters and lay there moaning. The moans gradually gave way to groans and then to screams. The excitable servants ran hither and yon. Were things not going well? Should she go to the hospital? Should a doctor or *M'tawa* be called? Well, shouldn't something happen? Everyone was in a state, where was Jewaher? They seemed like helpless children, unable to make a decision without her and she had gone visiting. It seemed that Bedur would not go to the hospital because she had been told they would strap her down on a table and yank the baby out from deep inside. It was a terrible place of magic and torture, no place for a baby to be born. But her screams continued all afternoon. Lindy and I felt as helpless as the servants. Bedur clasped Lindy's hand, her body wet with perspiration, her hair lank, her face contorted with pain, but she would not consider leaving her bed. We had no idea how to summon help. Finally, Lindy convinced one of the chauffeurs to go to Jewaher. She strode in, all five feet of her, assessed the situation quickly and, brooking no argument, had her bundled into the car and hustled off to the hospital where she very shortly gave birth to a lovely little daughter who soon became the centre of attention. Every day she is brought, all dressed in her best, to Jewaher to be held and kissed and shown off to visitors. All babies are adored by Arabs of all ages.

We all went to a baby shop exactly like one in the States except that the assistants are all men, and had great fun selecting gifts for the baby. Laila is to be her name, isn't that pretty? There is another Laila here too. So many people have the same name that it's very confusing. There must be a dozen Mohamets in the place.

I want to get this off today and we are going visiting, so I will stop here darling. I love and miss you very much, as you well know.

Mom

Saudi Arabia
Don't know the date

Hi Pat,

You are probably getting ready to go back to work after the long summer vacation. It's a good thing I didn't sign a contract for the new school year as I'm not sure how long I am going to be here. Originally I came to stay a month, but that was almost two months ago. Whenever I broach the subject they just wave it off, and since I am having a marvellous time in spite of a million frustrations, I guess I shall stay a while longer. Actually, I can't leave until they get me an exit visa. I didn't know about this when I arrived. You need a visa to get in, but you also need one to get out! I was a little startled when I learned this and don't know exactly how it works yet, but shall keep you informed. I hope you are all getting my letters! The other day I saw five letters I had given to Hamdi *three* weeks ago to mail. He forgot all about them. I have no idea how many others have been lost or forgotten. Also, in the two months I have been here I still have not received one word from the outside world! Are we still at peace?

Well, enough complaining for today, I'm going to fill you in on a little more of everyday life around the harem.

There are two western additions to the lives of the members of the harem: television and the telephone. Jewaher has two lines in her quarters, but just try to get one. The oldest princess and the seventeen-year-old prince appear to have grown a metal and plastic extension to their arms. They spend all their waking hours talking to friends. It is so bad that their father decreed that the phones are not to be used from 11:00 p.m. to 11:00 a.m. and so promptly at 11 o'clock each night, no matter who is on the phone to whom, you will be cut off mid-sentence as the lines are disconnected.

There is a large television in every room, as well as a video tape machine and stereo component. Video tapes of American films, some dubbed, others not, are rented for about $30. It is a thriving business. Arabs pack the shops every night to select their evening's entertainment. How some of these tapes pass the censors I don't know. They come home with four to five tapes each day. The tapes are of incredibly poor quality and are almost completely worn out very quickly. The sound track is so bad that very little can be understood and the 'snow' is so thick that I can't watch them even if I wanted to. The youngsters, however, spend every night in front of the set. The selection of tapes is generally left to the male driver who goes into town and picks them up for the family. I believe the shopkeeper just thrusts a handful at him and off he goes. They are definitely not our finest offerings. 'Disco Queen', 'Roller Derby', low-budget sci-fi, horror films, bad westerns. These movies give Arabian women and children their view of American life. After seeing 'Roller Derby' all the young people, from the twenty-seven-year-old Gada to the four-year-old Saad, had roller skates. Round the courtyard and driveway they went, falling down, scraping knees, but at least getting some fresh air and exercise. They were, however, very sceptical of me when I turned down all offers to join them. They are quite sure, after seeing the picture, that all Americans, when not hot-rodding, motorbiking, or zooming the sands on our dune buggies, propel ourselves from here to there on roller skates. What I said obviously didn't carry much weight; after all, they had seen it on American films.

When they saw a film featuring dune buggies they asked their father to buy them each a buggy, and . . . you guessed it . . . seven dune buggies coming up. This time only the boys will have them, girls do not drive.

I made a few caustic comments about the fact that in America I drove my own car and appreciated being able to take care of my own needs. Having to always wait until some male is free or in the mood to drive you to the store, or to go for you, is a constant irritant. Each person has his or her own chauffeur but it is surprising how skilfully these drivers manage to absent themselves when you want them. They have a cushy life, believe me. They are privy to so many of the indiscretions and private activities of the people they drive that they can do just about as they please. It would be disastrous for Gada, for example, if Hamdi were to mention to her father that he had driven her to a meeting in the supermarket instead of to her friend's home. My remarks about my ability to drive my own car at home elicited the explanation that of course they were sure a woman was capable of learning to drive, but after all, how would she be able to see where she was going behind her veil? Well, at least that was better than their reason for why I couldn't learn their card game.

On several occasions they have found themselves with hard-core porno films and I was amazed and amused to see Jewaher, her friends, servants, and the children of all ages gathered around, eyes glued to the set. They couldn't understand the words, but they could certainly understand the actions.

After seeing such films Jewaher looked at me with . . . what? . . . new respect? Well, if they saw it in our films, that's how it is in America. I feebly protested that I had never even seen the films, far less indulged in the antics! Once again they were very sceptical. At any rate, Prince Abduraman may have found that things have picked up in the harem since then!

As everything is strictly censored in Saudi, I have no idea how they get away with selling these ghastly tapes. The public television is so well censored that it's very humorous to watch. Films for general viewing are all family fare and every time even the most proper of husbandly pecks is about to be bestowed there is a 'bleep' on the screen as the action is cut, making a series of a very jerky movements on the part of the actors. I do believe Roy Rogers would not even be allowed to kiss Trigger. The censoring leads to some pretty incoherent films, but no one here seems to notice that great chunks have been removed.

Since Saudi women may not appear on television (it's difficult to emote with a veil over your head, I imagine) Arabic programmes are brought in from Kuwait or Egypt. They have their daily soap operas, and just as in America, the Arabian housewife or princess sits glued to her set. These films, meant to be heavy drama, are highly hilarious to the western viewer. Arabians are, under all circumstances, given to extravagant gesturing and wildly dramatic motions; when in front of a camera no holds are barred. These Egyptian Thespians are in seventh heaven as they give it all they've got. I'd like to say they are real hams, but being Muslims I suppose that would be somewhat inappropriate? Anyway, bosoms heave, eyes roll, breasts are clutched, people stagger, backs of hands are pressed tragically to foreheads, men and women alike sink to their knees to implore. Although I can't understand a word of the rapidly-spoken Egyptian, I can follow the story-line quite easily because of these histrionics. It is like watching our early silent films, only with plenty of noise. I always want to burst out laughing in the most tense and desperate moments, so I make many a mad dash from the room. My hostess sits spellbound, spitting seeds around her and sipping her tea.

Censorship is everywhere in Saudi and the people are told via public television only that which is considered good for them to know (which isn't much); a good deal of what is shown is religious in nature. There is much preaching, and every day we see the pilgrims in Mecca. The sight of the sacred Black Stone always brings a directive from Jewaher for me to look. I'm expected daily to express my amazement and delight. The people seem to have a very real affection and respect for their King. Even though the family is related to him, they seem awed every time he appears on the screen, which is at least once a day.

There is an English news broadcast every evening and the family is always eager for me to watch it. I remember the first night! They had told me to be ready, so at the appointed hour I hurried to take a seat close to the set. The children were 'shushed' and everyone courteously tried to maintain a semblance of quiet (you've no idea of the usual din) so I could hear clearly. First the commentator came on to say, 'Today his Royal Highness, King Khalid, sent messages of congratulations to the following people . . . he also sent condolences to the Prime Minister of Such and Such.' This was followed by a statement about oil production. I could hardly believe my ears, for this is the direct quote: 'Oil production will continue as it is, or less, or maybe more.' Not too elucidating, was it? Every day it is just about the same; first the messages from the King to other heads of state, and then a statement regarding the oil output for the day. The family is somewhat disappointed at my lack of enthusiasm for their English-language news broadcast. Lindy had chuckled when she found the family was going to get the English-speaking news for me, but simply said, 'Oh, yes, you must watch it.' Now I know why she never bothers to get it on her own set and had neglected to inform me of it earlier.

Actually, because the language ability of the announcer leaves quite a bit to be desired, there are frequent bloopers that lighten the day for American and British workers in far-off Arabia. One that still has people chuckling from time to time is the proud report that His Royal Highness had that day sent a letter of congratulations to Giscard-Mitterand on his erection! One really shouldn't miss a programme with opportunities for news like that!

Every piece of written matter that enters Saudi Arabia is censored, after a fashion. You take pot-luck when you invest in a magazine, for it may be wholly untouched or so cut about that you have a handful of confetti. The readability depends on the diligence of your friendly local censor. A conscientious one will remove, either with black marking pen or scissors, every reference to anything contrary to the teachings of the Koran and every picture of a woman's skin from the chin down. On one of our rare opportunities to select some reading matter I found a magazine with an article on tummy-trimming. When I returned home and settled down to read it I discovered, to my chagrin, that all the little figure diagrams had been scribbled out! On the other hand, if the censor is a lazy critter you may find almost everything intact but for a half-hearted scribble through one or two little items. For example, in another magazine I found the rather inoffensive neck of a hair stylist's model had been blacked out while on the next page a sensuous ad for intimate apparel had been left untouched. Ads for nylons, bathing suits and bras may be obliterated or left intact. It pays to peruse anything you want to buy very carefully.

The first glow of enthusiasm the young girls exhibited for showing off their country has definitely waned and other interests prevail. Perhaps there is nothing more to see in this sandy land. On the other hand, the delights of dragging an older lady around with you are probably no more enticing to a young Arabian girl than to an American one. Fun for a while, but soon it palls. And when it does the visitor is stuck . . . stuck behind the wall in a far land. Sounds dramatic? Yes, well, as the implications have slowly dawned, I find my emotions have changed. Annoyance lasted several weeks before it turned to frustration and gradually this has begun to work its way to fear and panic. How does one get out of here? Of course, dear Pat, in my usual understated fashion I am exaggerating the hell out of everything, but actually this exit thing is becoming a bit sticky. I can't just go out and pick up a visa and relying on the 'manana' approach of the Arab men is like relying on the stability of nitro-glycerine.

Say hello to Bill for me, though right now I'm not feeling too friendly toward the male sex. I think I'll get rid of some of this frustration by writing to a few of them and really telling them off, the chauvinistic characters. Poor ol' Ben wouldn't know what hit him, and Bob, having been here, would undoubtedly say, 'Aha, I told you so!' Ooooh, I just love that, they are so righteous and egotistical . . . funny I never noticed before!

Love ya,

Babs

Darling Trish,

As you can see, I am still here. Yesterday Jewaher said through Nura, 'Why do you want to go back America? In Saudia you have everything, you no work, you no need money, we give you anything you need.' It is a point I find hard to argue against without appearing rude. I asked again about my visa and was told they had misplaced my passport and so could not apply for it, but not to worry, they had just found it again and so would make application soon.

You will remember how loath you and I were to hand over our passports to the *concierge* when we were in Europe last year? Well here the Prince asked for mine immediately, saying it would be put in the safe for me. Now they tell me it was 'misplaced'. Maybe we Americans are a bit paranoid about our passports, but that seemed a bit much! 'Misplaced!'

Must stop complaining because really this *is* the life! Would you believe I haven't rinsed a nylon since I arrived here? I do brush my own teeth, but that seems to be the extent of my exertion.

For years the main diversion in the harem has been that of visiting. It has been the only way a woman could get beyond the wall without her husband, accompanied only by her male driver. Another woman's house is her sole access to the outside world. One doesn't just run next door in curlers and bedroom slippers for a cup of coffee in this land. Visiting is an art; it is a time consumer; it is a way to keep from going stark, raving mad behind the harem wall.

When a guest arrives, she comes complete with servants and three to six small children. She has spent hours carefully grooming, dressing in her newest gown and an array of jewels. Usually she brings a gift of fresh fruit, baked items, perfume, *oudh*, or material. It is more the planning and preparation for a visit that is of importance to the visitor than the visit itself, for once there it will be very dull. There will be the ceremonial kisses all the way around the room (never again will I be embraced so fondly by so many total strangers), then they will find a spot around the periphery of the room and be seated. If no men are present they will remove their veils. They will receive their cup of coffee and everyone else in the room will now switch from tea to coffee with them. They will have their servant bring in their little gift to be admired and they will probably then sink into silence until the next guest arrives. If a man comes, back go the veils. Men politely cough or stamp to give warning. The children will either sit staring at Lindy and me, or, if they have seen us before, will go out to play or watch the television. Babies will be passed around and then handed back to the servants to be watched.

Arabian women do not engage in small talk. There may be a few words of gossip exchanged if something of interest has transpired, but mostly they just sit and sip, sit and sip. After all, the 'Read any good books lately?' ploy is not much help when no one knows how to read. They do have one great source of conversation . . . their respective aches and ills, and oh, do they have them! Each one's pain and agony is greater than that of the other.

One day Jewaher was in seventh heaven; she could hardly wait for the first guest to put in an appearance. The day before she had been to the doctor, who had given her a sure-fire all-star attention-getter. She was to test her urine daily and take him a chart of its acidity or alkalinity on her next visit. When the guests arrived she hastily ordered one of the servants to bring a glass of urine and the magic paper. Everyone waited and watched with almost bated breath as, with a flourish that would do any vaudeville magician credit, she submerged the litmus paper in the fluid and watched it turn from blue to pink before their astounded eyes. Her gratification knew no bounds! Absolutely no one could top that one for the day! And for several days thereafter! The servants consumed a great deal of water around here to be ready for the summons, I can tell you!

As I become better acquainted with their ways I speculate on the reasons behind their lack of conversational gambits. The main one, of course, is the insular, restricted life they lead, but even so women can usually find something to chatter about. The Arabs are an extremely proud people and what others think of them is a great and constant concern to both men and women. Everyone must be very cautious not to give away any family secrets. I am, as a member of the family, constantly cautioned not to say anything about this or that, most of it so trivial in nature I would never think to repeat it anyway. This need to be thought perfect is a very definite and important aspect of the Arabian personality; they have a great fear of losing face. Neither do they want others to blame them for doing or saying something that would cause that other person's loss of face. All this leads to continual lying and evasion, another basic trait difficult for westerners to deal with or to fully understand.

Lest they be thought poor, the princesses hate to be caught in the same dress twice at any function beyond routine family activity. Material is selected daily for a never-ending production of new outfits. On holidays such as El Eid, which celebrates the end of Ramadan, as many as four or five dresses may be displayed, with shoes, jewels and purses carefully selected for each. When visiting, one must have a new dress; when giving a party the host family will change at least once during the course of the evening. For big parties and weddings the preparations take weeks. Gowns are often ordered from Europe. One young princess I met recently ordered her gown for a forthcoming important wedding from the London Couturiers who designed Lady Diana Spencer's wedding gown. She was delighted to report to all that she is paying $23,000 and, of course, would only wear it once! Price is of the utmost importance. I am constantly asked how much my dress, shoes, robe, bracelet or bangle costs. Invariably they ask if my jewels are real. Embarrassingly, I must usually say no, but it is embarrassing for them, not me!

Each sitting room in an Arabian household (and there are many sitting rooms) contains a large cabinet with row upon row of coffee and tea pots, all identical in design. Knowing that the very cheapest of these is at least $35 American, I totted up the number in one cabinet the other day. Thirty brass coffee pots and ten silver tea pots.

'Why do you have so many on display in every room? You never use them,' I said.

'Oh, if we didn't have them people would think we were poor!' explained Nura.

I laughed to myself for a while over this until Lindy pointed out that we are just the same with our little *objets d'art* and knick-knacks cluttering our tables and shelves, our pictures and wall hangings on every wall, our coffee-table books and curio cabinets. We are more subtle perhaps, but I'm not even sure about that. The traditional Arabian home is uniquely free of all these trappings, the coffee cabinet usually being the sole adornment. Exquisite cushions and rugs are the other source of opulence. All such items were used in the tents of the nomads; it was probably hard to hang a work of art in a tent.

Everyone does seem to have an inordinate fear that people may think they have less money than their associates. Each wants to have the biggest, the best, the most. Keeping up with the Joneses is a national occupation. They are the most insecure people I have ever known, in spite of their arrogant sense of their own importance. A strange anomaly, but then, when sudden wealth is poured on a poor nation what is one to expect? They want to impress a world that has formerly looked down on them that they are just as good as, or better than, anyone else; and they are all too aware they have nothing which will say so more convincingly than the things their money will buy. Is this such a strange human weakness? I think not. Can we forgive them this if they forgive our snobbishness? I rather feel the latter is a much more grievous fault and one that is in part directly responsible for the deep hatred the Arabs have for us. Oh yes, behind their exquisitely polite façade they do hate us for our continually tactless expressions of smug superiority.

To me the Arabs appear a sensitive people, loyal, proud, generous, volatile, and loving. They are not punctual; they may not be honest. They have a decided streak of cruelty interwoven with tremendous sentimentality. They have some of the strongest feelings of family responsibility in the world, and a real love for their country. They are confused and uncertain in a world which has many ways strange for them. When they accept you into their family they do so warmly;

you become one of them, and they want so much to be liked by you. But you must follow their ways.

Gada and Fatima have a young friend who is from a wealthy Syrian family living in their city. She is a frequent visitor but her ways and those of her family are not those of the Saudis. One day she arrived with beautifully-engraved invitations to her brother's wedding. There was one for Lindy and me. We always look forward to her visits for she is one of about four people who speak English quite well. We are actually able to carry on a conversation with her, ask questions and have her interpret the many things Jewaher, Lindy and I wish to say to one another. She had been talking of the wedding for days and begged us to come, explaining that it would be a Syrian ceremony, not Arabian, that there would be dancing and feasting, and best of all, the men and women would not be separated. It was to be held in one of the new hotels in town and I was dying to see the inside of the building, to say nothing of being eager to attend a Syrian wedding, and to mingle, after all these many weeks, with people of both sexes.

Jewaher, smiling and nodding, seemed pleased that we had been invited too. On the day of the wedding the three daughters informed us that because both men and women would be at the ceremony their father would not let them attend, but that we should certainly go. Jewaher again seemed delighted that we should attend, so we went about our preparations with excitement. The time for departure approached. I dressed in a new evening gown of fuchsia chiffon. Again Lindy loaned me a simply gorgeous necklace of diamonds and rubies set in gold with matching bracelet and rings. Not having pierced ears I had to pass up the earrings, but never have I been so bejewelled. Your sister, in a gown of black and gold, looked utterly beautiful. We waited for the chauffeur and cab. We waited, then waited some more. Finally Lindy sent a servant to Jewaher to ask what had happened to Mohammed, who had been told (we thought) to drive us to the hotel at 6:00 p.m. Word came back that Mohammed had to go out on an errand. With all the drivers they employed, they had sent him on an errand. They knew he was to take us to the wedding. Well! I asked if Hamdi could take us and was told that Hamdi was ill. What about the other drivers? All those Porsches, Cadillacs and Rolls Royces in the garage were mysteriously broken down and all the drivers were busy repairing them!

I walked back into the house to assimilate the lesson I had learned in Arabic diplomacy. They would never be so impolite as to come right out and tell me I could not attend the wedding. They went along with the game, but when the time came they successfully saw that we had no means of getting there.

Is it any wonder international politics involving the Arab world becomes so difficult? You *must* understand them, but this is not easy because our concepts of honesty and theirs of good manners are in conflict.

I've had the opportunity to attend several *Saudi* weddings so far. This whole area is undergoing much turmoil, as the surrounding customs are perhaps those most thoroughly divergent from our western ways. Each family unit handles the problems in a slightly different way, depending on the degree of westernisation or leniency of the head of the family. Many harried and worried fathers are simply reverting to the strictest possible interpretations of the Koran in order to block further inroads of disruption into their religious lives, leading to the erosion of their customs. Others are making concessions. It is a sad, alienating struggle.

The first wedding I attended was between Jewaher's brother, Prince of the blood royal, and a beautiful Bedouin girl. Prince Faisal had seen the girl, whose brother worked for him, but she had always been veiled. He had seen pictures of her, however, and realised her beauty extended beyond the lovely, graceful carriage he could observe beneath the veils. Laila had never seen him, but knew it was an honour to receive a proposal from this man of wealth and position. She knew he already had one wife. That was too bad; as do most of the women, she would have preferred to be his first, perhaps even his only wife. Still, that is the custom and there are many advantages to the system.

As the wedding day approached, Faisal was constantly in

and out of Jewaher's quarters in the harem. He was as nervous and excited as any young bridegroom in America. Jewaher took it upon herself to select a goodly supply of new underwear, socks and pyjamas for him. He actually blushed, this bearded, moustached, fortyish man, as he held them up for me to admire. He dashed in to show us the new shoes he had purchased, several pairs of fine Guccis, for which an alligator or two had given their all. He swooned, giggled and delighted in the teasings of Jewaher and his nieces and nephews. I couldn't refrain from asking him somewhat belligerently if his other wife would be at the wedding. I am very fond of her; she's shy, huge-eyed and sweet.

'Oh, no! I have sent her to the country to cry,' was his reply. It was said in a matter-of-fact tone and I could detect no twinkle in the eye to indicate he might be teasing the nosey American. The man was serious.

The preparations by our family were also quite extensive. Incense burners and coffee pots in blue velvet cases were sent to the mother of the bride, along with silver tea sets to be used and returned after the wedding. We selected gifts from the many items the gypsies brought to the house and we all had new gowns made or purchased from one of the elegant boutiques in town. The young princesses, Lindy and myself decided to buy 'off the peg' while Jewaher and the servants selected to accompany us, had theirs made. The day before the ceremony was spent in grooming our hair, nails, faces and bodies. Henna was slathered over every head; hands and feet were decorated in elaborate patterns of henna stain; all the body hair was most painfully removed with a gummy substance that is smeared on and yanked off by a woman skilled in this procedure. Even the nostril hair is removed (with which I suddenly discovered I am unfortunately generously endowed). Bodies were oiled and perfumed, hair set, nails painted. At last the time arrived. We managed, as usual, to present ourselves an hour late. As we were the guests of honour and everything had to wait until we arrived, you would think that was very rude and very hard on the mother of the bride. She seemed to take it smilingly in her stride, however. Everybody is always late for everything here; sometimes several *days* late.

As there is no liquor, no men, 'hundreds' of little children, and a terrified bride, these weddings are more of an interesting experience than a fun-filled evening, but interesting they certainly are if you don't have to attend more than one or two.

To begin with, the ceremony does not take place between the bride and groom. Can you believe that the bride isn't even *there*? It takes place between the groom and the *father* of the bride! The bride doesn't see her husband-to-be until he is a husband-that-is! So, I have not actually seen a wedding either, come to think of it. As a woman I am not allowed at the male ceremony. I wait along with the bride and other women until the marriage has taken place.

After the ceremony there are two parties, one for the women and children, and the other for the men. When we arrived at this wedding we were escorted by the mother of the bride to a small private sitting room where the bride sat in state with her attendants, three flower girls in western dresses with garlands of artificial flowers in their hair. The bride could be honestly described as pleasingly plump, and her face was truly beautiful. Her large, liquid black eyes stared at me with a look I have rarely seen in my life except in a couple of caged animals. I can only describe it as a look of sheer terror. She sat there stiffly in an American-made white wedding gown. The utilitarian straps of a large cotton bra showed through the delicate organza of a dress obviously intended for a equally delicate and strapless undergarment. This little inconsistency of grooming, of which she was so unaware, made her somehow touching and vulnerable to me. It was not of concern to anyone else, however, but simply another example of the incongruities that arise as one culture tries to adapt to another.

As members of the groom's family we were given seats of honour in the room with the bride, I soon discovered I had the only camera in the place, so with their delighted permission I began to take pictures of everything. But try though I might, I simply could not coax one smile of nuptial happiness from the frightened little face beneath the white veil. A long procession of women and children came and went, offering their congratulations. Since Laila spoke not a word of English I was sorely tempted to offer my condolences . . . having seen the groom . . . but I conquered it.

After everyone had greeted the bride we were invited to eat. Again we were taken to a small private room for the family where a cloth had been spread on the floor. Here we were served the traditional whole sheep on a bed of rice, with huge bowls of fruit and pudding. At Jewaher's house the lamb or mutton is always roasted to an invitingly crunchy brown, but here it had apparently been boiled, for it was a sickly, waxen-looking yellow that was definitely not tantalising.

We all squatted down in our Balenciagas and diamonds and proceeded to attack the thing. It was a very greasy activity, with no utensils and no napkins pandering to my western sensibilities this time. At its conclusion everyone had grease running in rivulets around their wrists, but their laps were immaculate. Alas, mine was splattered liberally wih fat droplets as usual. *How* do they do it?

The meal was followed by hand washing all round and a generous dousing with perfume. The *oudh* that Jewaher had sent to Laila'a mother was burning in braziers which the servants knelt to place beneath our skirts. This is a very common practice. They love the smell and when the smoke starts to billow up from the neck of your dress to envelop your head you are apparently 'done'. I am always extremely nervous at having these live coals held under my nylon slips. I have no desire to immolate myself for the sake of a quaint custom, but they are insistent so I clench my hands and bravely endure.

Once fed, perfumed and refreshed it was time to return to the still patiently-seated bride to await the coming of the groom. I was told that when he did appear he would be accompanied by one male attendant under the age of eighteen.

Suddenly I was startled by the pounding of drums and the tinny sound of tambourines. The hallway was filled with women and children waiting to catch a glimpse of the groom, but standing at the door were eight heavily-veiled gypsy women holding the tambourines and drums covered with animal hide. They heralded the bridegroom's arrival. As he swept into view, his white *thope* covered by a fine wool cape of brown piped in gold, the women set up a high-pitched tongue-wagging yell I had never heard before. It is a unique sound, very loud, very shrill, and I have never been able to duplicate it. Everyone joined in.

Prince Faisal swept majestically into the hall and, smiling broadly, entered the room where his bride, the beautiful Laila, sat transfixed. She looked numb, in an almost hypnotic state. After the couple had received individual greetings and best wishes from the women and children, they rose and joined the crowd assembled on the roof, where thirty carpets had been laid out.

Most Arabic homes have a roof garden where the women may sit in the cool of the evening. It is divided by a lattice-work screen and the men of the family entertain their friends on the other side. In this case the men's celebration was in the courtyard below.

The bride and groom sat on a raised dais with a huge tapestry of Mecca behind them. This same type of tapestry was the backdrop for the couple at each wedding I have attended. They sat there together for about an hour, during which time the women danced for them individually and in small groups to the music provided by the gypsies. A few of the Arabian women are good dancers; for the most part the best I can say is that they are uninhibited. Suddenly I spotted Jewaher under full sail and bearing down on me with an unmistakable gleam in her eye. 'Oh dear God,' I groaned. 'They expect *me* to dance!' I was never so right. Even without this I was feeling totally conspicuous. As relatives of the groom we were not wearing our veils and with my pale hair and fair skin it was taking all my Yankee brashness just to sit there and be stared at. The children were daring each other to sneak up and touch my hair, and as each child darted breathlessly past, snatching wildly as they went, I was beginning to look as if I'd been caught in a windstorm. What to do? I could politely decline until they finally stopped coaxing, thus appearing a poor sport and embarrassing the family, or I could go out there in front of two or three hundred strangers and make a complete ass of myself. I opted for the latter. My face burned and I felt the perspiration begin, but I guess the decision was the right one, for Jewaher and the girls were proprietorially proud of my low-class bumps and grinds. Maybe when I get back I can find work as the comedy relief in a girlie show? And where was your sweet sister all this time? Sitting there laughing her little head off at my discomfiture.

After the dancing, Prince Faisal rose to join his male guests in the courtyard below. The women sat and drank tea and coffee for another hour or so as children sprawled out wherever they could find the room and fell asleep, exhausted from the excitement and the hour. I worked my way over to the lattice-work and peered down at the men. Just like a scene from a B-movie, I was the sloe-eyed harem girl silently watching from behind the screen. I kept expecting Ali Baba to pop out of a jug or Douglas Fairbanks, Jr. to leap over the wall brandishing his sabre. Robert Redford would suit me just fine!

It all looked as disappointingly dull as things on our side . . . a lot of men with traditional red checked cloths that remind me of an Italian restaurant on their heads (their *ghotras*), gravely dancing around in a circle arm in arm. This weird, almost hypnotic dancing that they do is something the Arab men seem absolutely crazy about. Driving down the streets of Riyadh or Al Khobar in the evening you will pass huge vacant areas where hundreds of men are gathered, arms linked together, forming row after row. They shuffle endlessly around and around the space in a simple little step in time to the music. Once in a while they add sword flourishes to this ritualistic dancing. In a society bereft of women I guess this takes the place of the disco. I long to introduce these men and women to the delights of a waltz or foxtrot and imagine what a torrid tango would do to those Islamic morals! The older women are a little too plump to handle the jitterbug, but maybe some good hard rock is what they need. The younger generation loves to have me join them in their attempts at American dancing. And I enjoy the exercise. Lindy has taught them all the latest steps.

There was, by the way, what I presume was an unusual end to this particular wedding. As the guests began to depart, the women hired to prepare the tea and coffee demanded an additional 1,000 riyals, which is about $300 American. There was a shouting match between her and the mother of the bride, who was not about to pay her another cent. Jewaher, rather inappropriately I thought, pulled out 500 riyals and handed it to her. The woman looked at it, tossed it on the ground and spat on it. She then plunked herself down in the middle of the remaining guests with her arms crossed and refused to leave. The wedding party pointedly resumed their conversations, ignoring the woman, which was actually very hard to do under the circumstances. The bride sat through all this in glassy-eyed oblivion, staring straight ahead as she had all evening, after a few horrified glances at her husband. Eventually someone handed the woman something and she left. With her departed the rest of the guests. The Arabic wedding is not my idea of excitement but that it is interesting one can't deny. It often has overtones of a Mack Sennet comedy.

The twenty-year-old Princess Fatima recently received a proposal. The young man was happily and monogamously married, so the story goes, to a lovely girl of excellent connections. They had a two-year-old child. One day the wife's milk-mother came to visit. She was horrified to discover that she had also been the milk-mother of the husband, making them brother and sister through the milk. Marriage between such a pair is strictly taboo. There was nothing to be done, so the broken-hearted wife took the baby and returned to the home of her father. The husband began his search for another wife. Being a devout young man, he asked the marriage broker to find him a good Muslim girl from a suitable family, one who would obey all the commands of the Koran. There would be no watching of television with its corrupting ideas and she would wish to observe *Purdah* (seclusion) faithfully.

The names of Fatima and Gada were on the list of possible wives as princesses from an impeccable branch of the family.

For reasons of her own, Gada declined the offer promptly. Fatima may accept it. That she would even consider it dumbfounds me. Fatima, the world traveller, who smokes in the privacy of her bedroom, who sneaks into hotel dining rooms and bowling alleys without her parents' knowledge, who argues for freedom and longs to drive a car, is actually considering this very seriously. She told me that if she does say a tentative 'yes', then they will exchange photographs. She has asked me to help her select a picture to send him in that event. If the picture exchange should be pleasing to both parties they will then be allowed to converse on the phone, to be sure they are of one mind about their marital expectations. If this brings continued agreement (someone will certainly be stretching their truths here) then within thirty days the marriage could take place. What makes Fatima even momentarily consider this marriage? The pressure to marry is very great here; it is the sole reason for a woman's existence. They move from the restrictions of life with father to the even more restrictive life of a Saudi wife. There is never a time in between to know what it is like to be on their own, unless, like Fatima, they have a father who has been lenient or foolhardy enough to allow them to leave the country and experience life beyond. Prince Abduraman, to his regret, allowed Fatima to accompany her English-educated aunt to London, Paris, Berne and Madrid. He didn't like what he saw upon her return and has told Nura she need not hope for a similar experience. She is to remain at home until married. She is very sad about this but at fourteen wouldn't dream of arguing with her father.

According to the Koran a man may have no more than four wives at one time, and then only if he can support them all in an appropriate style. Westernisation is making the idea of polygamy unattractive to the younger men, with monogamy becoming something of a status symbol, but plural marriages are still the primary pattern. That came as no surprise to me. Most of us know of the Koran's generosity to man; what I had not realised is that being allowed four wives *at one time* can keep the musical beds rolling at an amazing speed. One of the first men I met upon my arrival has merrily rotated his way through twenty wives, and still seems to be going strong. This old gentleman is Abduraman's father, very wealthy, very old. When we arrived at their home he was sitting in the courtyard, where all four of his present wives were gathered with him to meet me, along with a gaggle of small children. The Prince had only one eye, an empty socket giving evidence to his part in battle when he fought alongside Ibn Saud as a young man. His voice is high and he seems to cackle. All in all, he is not your every day Omar Sharif but he has four young and beautiful wives, two of whom are pregnant. He told me he expects to *keep* his latest bride, a very lovely eighteen-year-old, as she 'pleases him'.

I have asked many questions about this situation. Why in the ever lovin' *world* would those pretty young things marry an old man unless they were forced into it? But no, they are not forced, they have the right to refuse. Surely even life with father would be better than this? The phrase 'fate worse than death' was coined, in my humble opinion, for unions such as this. Obviously I would never make a gold digger. It was laboriously explained to me what a great honour it is for these girls to marry such a great prince, and when he tires of them, which experience shows doesn't take too long, he has to provide for them most liberally at the time of divorce. They can then set themselves up in their own homes with their own servants, and importantly, all children under the age of ten remain with their mothers. Then at last they will be free to travel, to do as they wish; most choose simply to remarry, perhaps next time for love?

Well, there are no problems of unwed mothers, destitute, abandoned women lining up for their welfare checks at the taxpayers' expense. Every woman is cared for and protected by either a father, husband or ex-husband. Also, as a Saudi citizen, she receives her monthly pension from the government as does every other Saudi from the age of seventeen months of age. I was surprised to discover the Arabian women control their own finances and have their own money. They have strong inheritance rights; this, coupled with their shares of the government oil royalties, makes them financially secure and independent. There is no poverty in Saudi. There seem only to be degrees of wealth.

There is another prince whom I see often, for he is Jewaher's father and comes almost daily to her harem quarters to eat his noon meal. He totters in with a cane and lowers himself painfully to the only chair in the room, which is kept especially for his use. Waited on devotedly by all, he is served a huge meal in solitary splendour. No men ever eat with the women.

He is said to have six huge boxes (safes, I presume) the size of refrigerators packed with riyals because he doesn't believe in banks. He is reputed to be incredibly rich and at present only has two wives. One morning when I put in an appearance in the Beige Room I was greeted by a cacophony of sound that, in the small room, almost split the eardrums. I recognised it as the shrill, tongue-wagging yell I had heard at weddings and all the servants, who had jumped up when I entered the room, were responsible for it. Old Jamal grabbed me and bestowed a dozen delighted kisses on each cheek. 'Mabruk, Mabruk,' she kept explaining. What in the world was up? Everyone was so happy for me, but no one seemed able to tell me why. Jewaher was beaming. Would no one ever arrive who spoke enough English to tell me what was going on? I didn't like the look of the intertwined finger gesture they kept making.

At last one of the uncles arrived to visit, a young man about thirty who was educated in California. 'Thank goodness,' I gasped, 'What *are* they all jabbering about?'

After a few brief words with Jewaher he smilingly explained that her father had expressed a willingness to make me his wife! I would be wife number *thirty-four*. Then the words and phrases everyone was shouting at me began to make sense . . . 'Amerika m'hoob quays, Saudia hellowa . . . floos kathir . . . mabruk, mabruk!' They were telling me that America was not very desirable while Saudi Arabia was beautiful. They offered congratulations because now, at last, I would be married and would be very, very rich. Now I would never want to go home!

This was beginning to sound like the 'Perils of Pauline' to

me. I really have a strong desire to end this letter here with the line 'to be continued next week . . .', just leaving you to wonder 'will she sell herself for six refrigerators full of paper money, or will our Nell remain virtuous and impecunious to the end?' Well, I figure his assets are definitely frozen, and besides that, he's the most decrepid old soul I've seen outside an old folks' home. I'd hate to be responsible for pushing his other leg into the grave. So *no go*, but how to get out of it tactfully? I told them I was already promised to an oil baron in Texas (they would understand that). I was somewhat chagrined and piqued to discover they were only mildly disappointed when I declined, and I get the distinct impression they have decided I am just not very bright. Well, some Americans might even agree.

Can you imagine the number of children that man must have? Each of Abduraman's wives has ten. Ibn Saud, who founded the kingdom, had 109 children, nine of whom are no longer alive. There are fifty-year-old people going to hospitals to visit a young wife of their father and taking a peek at their newest aunt or uncle. Tracing family trees and keeping relationships straight is extremely complex. I think everyone is trying to outdo old Ibn Saud; they are very proud of him and his physical prowess.

As I look at the lives of the women in *purdah*, and at those of the men whose comings and goings are above question, I am reminded very much of the way a man treats a favourite dog in our country. When he chooses to come home he expects to find Fido faithfully waiting. A couple of brisk pats on the head, a romp, a walk together at day's end, then the master is off to his own pursuits and Fido returns to his waiting. It seems a suitable simile. When we have a pet it is not consulted about its life style, but we attempt to provide well for it. Much money is spent on proper food, vitamins and shots. The dog may be sent to the doggie-parlour regularly to be clipped, shampooed and perfumed. It may wear a jewelled collar and even have an attendant who sees that it is walked and exercised every day. It is taken on trips and has its own special place to sleep. Some may even look forward to satin-lined coffins and fancy funerals. They are often pampered and petted more than many children, but when you get down to it, they are completely at the mercy and control of their owners.

The women in Arabia have so many restrictions while the men seem to have none. Can you believe that if a woman is not a virgin on her wedding night the groom may send her back to her family in disgrace? There are beautiful hotels, sports arenas, theatres, bowling alleys, swimming pools, restaurants of every description and a degree of glamour in all the major cities. A few of these establishments have gone to added expense and provided a separate family section where a man may take his wives, but most will cater only to the men.

It isn't lying around with nothing much to do all day that really upsets me; being waited on hand and foot after years of the great American rat race is marvellous. I'm almost frightened at the ease with which I've adapted to this indolent existence. No, what brings my blood to the boil is the thought that I am here doing nothing because a *man* decreed it, and the men may all be out partying. They just lock their women up (did I tell you there are actually guards at the gates and bars on all the windows?) and go about their business and pleasures. Their pleasures, I must admit, don't seem to be much more exciting than those of the women. They visit a lot too.

I have never thought of myself as a woman's lib advocate. I thoroughly enjoyed the attentions of the opposite sex. Flowers, candy, perfume, you betcha! And I have no desire at all to burn my bra, or insist upon opening doors. But *now* I am beginning to hate the sight of these arrogant creatures. Every time a white-clad male sails imperiously into the room, causing all the women to rise, I feel the resentment surge. Then, somewhat shamefacedly, I remember that all my life men have risen when I enter a room. It's just what you are used to, I guess.

Actually everyone is so very kind to me, and the men are the most courteous in the world. It's just that damnably frustrating idea that they can do things I am not allowed to. I think of all women in the world, we Americans are the least able to cope with the Arab way of life. And our beloved Lindy is a perfect example. She has at last confided to me that much as she loves Abdul Raman, she is afraid she will quite literally and simply lose her mind if she remains locked up in here much longer. She is going to ask him to return to America with her and the baby. The problem is that the American way of life was almost as difficult for him, and he has responsibilities here. She is afraid he won't go and will refuse to let her go unless she leaves the baby. Little Tarek is so adorable! One thing I worry about all the time is how he will ever learn to talk with such a polyglot assortment of languages around him. His nurse speaks Tagalog, his playmates speak Arabic; Lindy's maid speaks Thai; and his parents and I speak English! He seems to understand us all, but says only a few words himself. They are, however, in English.

Well, I shall keep you posted darling. Also, I am still eagerly waiting for the day when a letter manages to get through from you. You do write such delightfully chatty ones and I am so anxious for news of you.

Much, much love always,

Mom

Dear Bob,

What's new in the real world? Is Canada now a part of the Union? As for me, my Arabian Nights seem to be stretching on a little longer than I had anticipated. Not just sure when I shall see you again, maybe several weeks. The latest excuse for not being able to get my exit visa is that Yosseph, who handles such matters for the family, has gone to London on a brief business trip so it will have to wait until his return.

I seem to recall that when I was preparing to leave, you warned me I might have some difficulty getting out of here. However, the reasoning behind the jokes and gibes was somewhat different from stark reality. Everyone kept suggesting with great jocularity that all the rich sheiks would be beating a path to my tent, and I would not want to return to mundane old California. Ah, well, much as I should like to relate otherwise, nothing could be farther from the truth.

In the months that I have been here I have actually seen only a handful of men, for no one outside the family is invited to enter the women's quarters, and the places they take me to are definitely not geared for socialising between the sexes. I've met the uncles, the sons, and the grandfathers. That's it, with the exception of the male servants.

One thing I have trouble with is this custom of wearing a veil! Every time I think I have figured out when I do or don't need to wear it, someone changes the rules! I think I have figured it. Jewaher and her servants wear the veil at all times, wrapped around the head and falling loose down one side so it can be raised to cover the face quickly whenever a male over seventeen enters. If the man is a close relative of Jewaher's she does not raise her veil but her women do. The three young princesses, on the other hand, wear the veil only when they leave the harem or when a very important relative visits. This seems to hold true *unless* one of the women who comes to visit is of a higher rank and is very devout. In that case the veils suddenly put in an appearance and are very conscientiously raised the moment a man appears. The raising and lowering of these veils is done with a languorously graceful motion of the hand that is very attractive and enticing to watch. As for me, however, I always seem to be fumbling for mine with the clumsiest of gestures. I couldn't attract a marine on leave from a combat zone! Another thing that happens only when a devout visitor is present is the observance of the daily prayer rituals. Good Muslims, as you know, go through a ritualistic washing followed by kneeling and praying five times a day. They now have prayer rugs with little compasses and plastic location-finders so that no matter where the faithful may roam, they can always point their prayer rug, and consequently themselves, directly at Mecca. Jewaher and Abduraman rise every morning at 3:00 a.m. to begin their day with prayers. Their children are usually not even in bed yet, and prayers are the last thing on their minds. Let their aunt, Princess Nura, arrive, however, and you can be sure that come pray-time everyone will be on their knees, fannies pointed skyward as they press their foreheads devoutly to the ground.

Despite the fact that the young people, like young people everywhere, are very lax about their religious devotion and are showing their rebellion toward the traditions of their parents, the family is definitely strong and important here. I envy their closeness and sense of love and responsibility to one another. America's fragmented families have lost so much. These people know that no matter what happens to them they may always expect support from the family. It is a deeply entrenched solidarity bound up in the religious teachings of their Koran. For me, it is truly delightful to experience, as an accepted member of this family, the lack of concern for age division that seems to plague westerners. The family spends much of every day together. Though one or two of the older ones may be off visiting friends or shopping for a few hours, they will soon all turn up. When one does go shopping, he or she will almost always think to bring home a toy or a sweet for the younger children. When they return from a trip away they do so laden with gifts for everyone. Even I have received presents of material from people returning from Jeddah or London, for example. They don't forget anyone.

In the evenings when we are all gathered together they love to have me join in their activities. It delights them that I will teach them new dance steps and try to learn theirs, that I will play cards and show them exercises. Although Jewaher is always there, and often the Prince as well, they are only benign onlookers. Only very rarely will Jewaher bestir herself to join in anything, but she is there, and the family is together.

This charming family togetherness was even more apparent when they took me out to see their ranch. It is an enormous one located several hours' drive from the city. As we were to spend several days there, it was quite an expedition. Surely Admiral Byrd set out for the Pole with less commotion and preparation than went into our little excursion! First we had to decide which of the many servants would accompany us, then how many cars we would need, what clothing, toys, special foods, and so on. Despite the fact that every member of the family has his or her own private car, it is again indicative of their enjoyment of each other that when everyone is going they much prefer to cram themselves into one vehicle. The cars are air-conditioned, but you can expect just so much help for ten people packed like sardines into a Mercedes in 130° weather. My idea of true torture. I heard this joke in the States: 'Why were there only 500 Indians at the battle of the Little Big Horn?' Answer: 'They all came in one car.' It comes to my mind every time I watch this crew piling in or out of a car! One night when we went to a special ladies' night at the fair I counted eighteen bodies in one limousine. And please remember these women are not, repeat not, size 10 . . . or even 12 or 14 or 16!

We were well into the desert, *en route* to the ranch, when Jewaher announced that it was time to pray. Stop the car, untangle arms and legs, burst out onto the hot sands. Servants quickly spread the prayer rugs and everyone faced Mecca. Here I learned that when the Arab is in the desert, far from water, he still ritualistically 'washes' the hands, face and head by using the sand of the desert. It was a moving moment as they carefully explained to me how it was done, and even the

90

four-year-old knelt in the heat of the day on the hot, arid ground.

Once back in the car I settled down to indulge in serious misery. There was no lady-like glow; I was drenched in sweat, cramped, squeezed and filled with self-pity. The itch that had developed behind my left ear had little hope of being scratched by a hand buried somewhere beneath the soft folds of feminine flesh pressing against me from all sides. Voices, shrill with excitement, assailed my ears in a never-ending, ever-louder jabber of Arabic. I was sure I'd expire long belong I ever had a chance to glimpse our destination. Even the sight of groups of camels ambling across the dunes caused little more than a half-hearted gasp of appreciation.

After an eon of time that my watch insisted was little over an hour, we turned off the main highway onto their land and drove about ten miles along a wide gravel road to the first gate. At this point I noticed a large sign (in Arabic of course) inviting passers-by to help themselves to water at the ranch. I liked that; it was so typical of gentle, quiet Abduraman.

Another couple of miles and suddenly out of the desert appeared the traditional wall, but it had blended so well I was almost upon it before I saw it. Once inside Jewaher's gate it was a fairyland of loveliness, with marble walks, formal gardens and fountains. There are four gates, one for each of the wives as well as the Prince. There were four large main buildings, again for each of the wives and the Prince, and in addition, cookhouses, laundries and various servants' quarters. They have their own generator and a mosque complete with loudspeaker so the Prince can call his people to worship.

Jewaher's home has private bedrooms and baths for each of her children and guests; her quarters; a formal dining room (apparently only for show, just like the one in the city); the actual eating room; the formal living room ringed with overstuffed brown chairs and couches; the mouth-wateringly luscious oriental carpet, elegantly thick and inviting to the foot; and the sitting room that contained wall-to-wall carpeting and was ringed with cushions. I wish I knew what Abduraman's was like, for you can be sure his would be even grander as is the case in all Arabic homes, for that is the place shown off to male visitors. I was not invited to inspect it, however. Nura, Fatima, Lindy and I went over and tried like schoolgirls to sneak in for a peek when the Prince was out with his foremen, but even then it was securely locked.

In addition to the buildings and gardens there is a fabulous little playland for the young children of the three wives. It has many rides, including a miniature train that will take you on a ride through the grounds, a merry-go-round, swings, and a ferris wheel. Our little Tarek had a ball. One memory I will take with me most fondly is that of Princess Jewaher squealing with delight as she came zooming down a high, cork-screw slide, her long dress up around her ears, her fat little thighs exposed for all the Muslim world to see.

There is also an interesting replica of an old time Bedouin sitting room that the Emir had built near the edge of a cliff to look out over the vast expanse of his ranch and farmland. A large, three-sided tent-like affair, it has a sunken pit for heating tea and water, huge clay water jugs, and colourful cushions.

On the ranch are many head of cattle, sheep, goats and chickens. They also keep several horses which they purchased especially for my daughter to ride when she is there, but no one else rides them, a fact I find quite surprising, don't you? They also have many fruit trees and an enormous farm where most of the fruit and vegetables for the family are grown.

The swimming pool was a dream come true . . . built again close to the cliff edge so that you can look out over the desert through high archways. While we were there the moon was full and very beautiful, it shone through the arches onto the water, turning it to silver. At the opposite end of the enormous pool is a covered area which gives shade when sitting and drinking the tea and coffee brought from the house on silver trays. The bath houses are also at this end. An aqueduct carries the pool water out to irrigate the fields below.

The water, crystal clear and pure, was heated by the desert sun to a perfect temperature. No need for chlorine and other chemicals in this private pool fed by mountain streams. We stayed in the water for hours. The strange thing is that since Arab ladies may not show their thighs, they all went swimming in their underwear and long slips – much more revealing when wet than my one-piece bathing suit, and believe me, not in the least conducive to the development of the fine art of swimming. Not surprisingly, therefore, none of them do swim and they are greatly impressed by the aquatic skills of my daughter. Lindy, having grown up by a lake, and with a swimming pool at hand, swims like a mermaid. The family loved to watch her do swans, jack-knives, and somersaults off the diving board, and would clap, cheer and call for more. Even hampered by a long clinging skirt, I had to admit she looked terrific, if a bit too slender these days for my maternal approval.

Then it was my turn. No match for Lindy's graceful finesse, I neverthelss grew up around water too, and am at home in it. I dived in and swam the length of the pool, luxuriating in the unaccustomed exercise and that absolutely marvellous water. As I stood up at the shallow end, everyone jumped in to cluster around me. 'Mom can swim! Mom can swim!' They were all shouting in wild excitement. Jewaher stood at the very edge of the pool clapping her hands and beaming with delight. Everyone begged me to assist Lindy with some lessons, and we all madly flailed around, having a glorious time, far into the starry night.

Life at the ranch is much more relaxed than it is in town. Jewaher and Abduraman have no need to maintain their positions, there is not the steady stream of visitors and family comings and goings. 'Appearances' are not so important here. Everyone exhibits a carefree, happy exuberance that made me wonder why they didn't spend a great deal more time in this heavenly spot, where I could wear slacks and tramp around. The youngsters have motor bikes, cycles, and some strange horribly dangerous three-wheeled contraptions that keep threatening to tip over as the young men tear around on them. The girls also donned jeans and raced up and down the desert roads on their motor cycles. There were many falls into the ditch, lots of tears and cuts, but thankfully, no broken bones. Fifteen-year-old Saud took me for a wild ride on his motor cycle and I discovered too late that I didn't know the Arabic word for 'STO-O-O-P'.

They have just completed a new building, their outdoor sitting room. Octagonal in shape, it replaces the huge Bedouin tent I understand stood there before. It is glass on all eight sides; carpeted, draped, and fully air-conditioned. All done in a soft, clean green with touches of rose, it is cool, comfortable and refreshing.

How I hated to see our visit there come to a close! For one thing it was the first exercise I have had in two months, as well as being so unforgettably beautiful. Abduraman left his other two wives behind on this trip, which was made for my entertainment, and Jewaher was ecstatically happy and rather smug wearing a little pussycat smile all day. Despite what they say there is considerable jealousy between the wives. They also send their children to spy on one another, and Abduraman often has to lecture them on their behaviour toward each other and to their respective children. Then they will do something ostentatious to impress him, such as buying new dresses for the daughters of the other wives, or sending a special *oudh* to their house in a fancy package. I find them disarmingly transparent in so many ways.

One night while at the ranch we spread carpets out on the lawn in the rose garden and had a sort of picnic supper, just Jewaher, the Prince, three daughters, Lindy and myself. It was a beautiful evening and for the first time I saw Jewaher flirting unabashedly with Abduraman. He loved it and responded with good humour, laughing and joking, and even pinching Jewaher lovingly. He shyly attempted a few words in English that I know he must have spent much time practising. Nura and Lindy were kept busy trying to translate for all of us as we had the longest, most intimate conversation of my stay. It was indeed a magic spot that seemed to transform us all.

At home Jewaher can be something of a martinet, with a truly formidable temper. When I hear the screams and shrieks emanating from her sitting room I always steer clear until things calm down. She wears heavy wooden clogs which she throws with great force and unerring aim at whoever has offended her. When our plump little princess reaches for that shoe, I instinctively duck, but it amuses me that she can mete out punishment without ever getting up. In spite of these frequent outbursts, which inevitably bring severe physical pain to someone, everyone loves her. Perhaps they realise the great pressure she is under in keeping that huge establishment running smoothly. She suffers from high blood pressure and despite her generosity and great kindness, when people irritate her beyond a certain point she erupts. It never lasts long and she never holds a grudge against the wrongdoer. They in turn seem to hold no grudge against her for their bruises.

Bob, all the many tips and bits of information you gave me regarding life over here, the feelings of the people, the restrictions and frustrations I would encounter, have indeed been most helpful. When I return we shall have to have the longest koffee klatch in history to exchange and compare notes. I'm keeping a little notebook of daily experiences so there will be no escaping every single little detail; aren't you lucky?

Love to you, as always,

Babs

Dear Pat,

Because of the language barrier I am not always as cognisant of what is going on around here as I would like to be. The nuances escape me and sometimes even the big picture, as was the case this week when a near-tragic event erupted seemingly without any provocation.

I had gone to bed about 1:00 a.m. and was sleeping soundly when a servant burst into my room. A stream of excited Arabic poured out. 'Shwy shwy,' I broke in as I hastily grabbed my robe, 'slowly, slowly.' Her first two words, 'Emira Jewaher,' were spoken slowly then she was off again, rattling away and dragging me by the hand. It didn't take an interpreter to tell me something was wrong. We ran the distance from my house to Jewaher's across the open courtyard. When I arrived I found about twenty-five hysterical men, women and children wringing their hands, wailing and shouting. They parted quickly as I arrived and I darted through to arrive at Jewaher's bedside. She lay there in a comotose condition, breathing heavily through her mouth. What was wrong? Her servant held up three empty bottles found beside the bed: Valium and two bottles of sleeping pills. I didn't know how many she had taken altogether, but it certainly appeared to be enough to render her unconscious. My medical experience, based primarily on television series such as 'Marcus Welby' and 'General Hospital', told me we had to get her up on her feet and keep her walking around. The shows didn't tell me how to accomplish this feat when the victim is over 300 pounds of unconscious fat! Lindy arrived, sized up the situation immediately, sent for the car, told Nura to call the hospital, and then indicated to the two largest, and hopefully, strongest males that they were to get her off the bed and on to her feet! It would have been difficult even under ideal conditions, but with six hysterical princes and princesses all trying to help by grabbing her arms, head, hair, anything they could get a grip on, it was all but impossible. Despite the seriousness of the situation, I could not help but appreciate the humour of it. The Arab men seem to be as excitable and emotional in a crisis as the women. Progress was hampered once they had her upright by the family and servants grabbing at her legs from both front and rear, trying to be helpful and only creating chaos. It took some real lung power on my part to get everyone out of the way so they could proceed. Then we came to the doorway, a bottleneck that successfully stopped the crowd's forward impetus. First they pulled, then they pushed, finally they turned sideways, and tugging, pushing, pulling and dragging, succeeded in getting through the door, plop! Then came the steps. Everyone swarmed around again and this time they managed to lift her, three or four to a leg. At last they were at the car, huffing, puffing, sweating. Jewaher's head lolled on her shoulders; she moaned softly, her eyes rolled upward. Somehow this wild mob succeeded in shoving her into the car, then – I could hardly believe my eyes – everyone piled in, servants, children, youths. No one would be left behind! Lindy and I decided the hospital attendants could take over and quietly returned to my room to await the news Nura had promised to relay by phone.

A few hours of fitful sleep crept by and Lindy was summoned to the phone. Nura's relieved voice told us all was well and while Jewaher was to remain in the hospital for a few days, they would all be home shortly.

In the next few days I realised how important Jewaher's presence was to the smooth running of the palace. Meals were served two hours early or an hour late, they were skimpy and poorly served. No one arrived to make the morning tea and coffee and there was a general scarcity of servants as they all took little vacations from their duties. The laundry was not done, no carrot juice was to be had; suddenly we were out of oranges. Gada, who was supposedly in charge, was ineffectual. The younger princelings, who spent most of their time fighting or crying anyway, seemed to caterwaul even more and got on my nerves increasingly. No one dared to correct or discipline them but Lindy, and no one was there to hand out a steady stream of money for goodies whenever they cried now. Their phoney tears of princely misery went unrewarded much of the time. I couldn't help feeling it was exactly what they needed, but their constant wailing was setting my teeth on edge. I have long felt that Jewaher's brand of child-rearing leaves much to be desired. We hear so much about pampered princes, and it is definitely true!

We didn't spend much time at home in the four days that the Princess remain in hospital, however. After a few hours of sleep on the morning that Jewaher was taken there, we all prepared to pay her a first visit. After much rushing around for forgotten items and much shouting of 'Yella, yella!' (let's go) two carloads of people took off for the hospital. Used to the American routine of two to four visitors at a time, twenty-minute stays and rigid visiting hours, I was in no way prepared for what followed.

When we arrived, I found Jewaher ensconced in one of the suites that are reserved for royalty at the big beautiful new hospital. Four or five servants sat on the floor; Prince Abduraman sat by her bed reading his inevitable newspaper; flowers were everywhere; huge containers of coffee and tea were set up to serve guests. We poured into the rooms, filling her bedroom and the small sitting room. Kisses all round, then we settled down on couches and floor to assimilate the excitement of this occasion. Jewaher seemed somewhat wan but otherwise quite well. She accepted graciously the additional flowers, perfume and candy we had brought. Pointedly, nothing was said as to the circumstances that had led to the present situation. I felt as though I were at a huge tea party.

Not too long after we all arrived other family and friends, always accompanied by servants, and often by several small children, began arriving. People came and went, coffee and tea flowed. Children cried, whooped with laughter, ran madly up and down the halls; grown-ups chatted, delighted at this unexpected opportunity to get out from behind the wall, to see other surroundings, to be a part of the general excitement. The hospital kitchens were called to send up platters of sand-wiches and *hors d'oeuvres*. Jewaher had obligingly provided several hundred people with a marvellous source of entertain-ment. By now I felt as if I were a spectator at a three-ring circus.

After a few hours of this, the kitchen were again called and dinners were ordered for forty-five people. I couldn't believe it. Neither could the hospital, apparently, for shortly thereafter a somewhat harried young intern came in to view proceedings. Most of the staff of the hospital is English-speaking. Doctors, nurses and technicians are primarily American, British, Australian and Canadian, although there are also many Germans, some French and some Indian, as well as a smattering of other nationalities. The young intern was British. Spotting me, he came over with a relieved look.

'Can you tell me how long everyone will be staying and how many will be here tomorrow?'

'I'm afraid I must say I have absolutely no idea to both questions,' I answered sympathetically. 'I am totally amazed and not a little horrified at the entire spectacle.'

'We really aren't equipped to handle large dinner parties without any pre-arrangement,' he said worriedly.

At this point Fatima came over to find out what was going on. I explained that usually people who are sick do not have so many visitors and that they usually stay only a short time. Fatima was furious! Drawing herself up and flinging back her long tresses she glowered at the poor young doctor. She shouted in accented but fully understandable English, 'You do not ever tell the family of a Prince what to do!' Then, brooking no protestation, she turned and strode off. The doctor scuttled out thoroughly abashed. I wasn't too sure how much of Fatima's haughty anger had been meant for the doctor and how much of it was meant for me. We spent between seven and ten hours at the hospital each day. Somehow, in spite of us, Jewaher recovered and returned home yesterday. Trying not to look at it through western eyes, perhaps this family-oriented woman, so used to the noise and hubbub of relatives, friends and servants coming and going endlessly, would not have recuperated at all had she been left alone for large portions of the day in the sterile sanitation of the hospital. Who can say?

In some ways they are so totally different from us and yet in other ways so very much alike. I remember getting such a chuckle last month from something one of the young aunts told me. It seems that during Ramadan certain people do not have to fast; pregnant women, old people, babies, the sick, and menstruating women, for example: So-o-o, what do these clever ladies do? They tell their husbands that during Ramadan their periods are seven days long! They may fool their husbands, I'm not too sure about Allah.

Their open, almost crude approach to sexual matters often causes me to turn a somewhat hot and prickly red. The other day I made several trips out of the room because I was exasperated with the obnoxious behaviour of little Prince Hamud. Jewaher was sitting with her father and two of the young uncles, when suddenly she became aware of my comings and goings.

'What is the matter, do you have the blood?' she called out.

Everyone looked at me. It was my last trip out of the room!

Another time I entered the room to find one of the guests, a large lady who appeared to be about forty-five or fifty, was going from person to person holding out a huge bared breast for everyone to squeeze.

'What in the world is she doing that for?' I queried in a low voice to one of the girls.

'Everybody say she have baby, so she show no milk, breast soft.' When she came to me I solemnly squeezed, and shook my head in agreement.

'No baby,' I said.

She smiled triumphantly at the assemblage and sank back down to the floor.

Another incident that left me somewhat startled occurred when we were discussing the method of removing hair from the body by means of the sticky substance they smear on and rip off. Jewaher wanted me to understand that they remove all body hair, and to be sure I understood exactly what she meant, she suddenly reached out and grabbed the ankle of the old story-teller sitting near by. Giving a great jerk, she hauled the woman over on her back, flipped up her skirts, and pulled down the voluminous long pantaloons they wear beneath the skirts. There for my edification was proof positive that when she said all body hair was removed, she meant *all* body hair! The poor woman was somewhat discomfited, but not as much as one would expect given the number of people sitting around. Everyone roared with laughter.

Hair is very important to Saudi women, the lack of it on the body and a plentitude on the head. Their beautiful, thick, long and shining tresses are their crowning glory and they play a very important role in the lovely dances of the Arabic women. It is alluring to watch as they move slowly and gracefully to the music, turning their heads from side to side in such a way that the hair spreads out like a raven fan. Then in another step it is tossed vigorously to cascade first down one shoulder and then the other. When they attempted to teach me their dances it was obvious immediately that it could never be done effectively with my head of hair, too short, too thin, too fair.

They spend considerable time caring for their hair, henna being the main agent. They apply the henna, hot towels, and disappointingly, wrap themselves in plastic caps such as you find in any neighbourhood beauty shop in the States. Somehow I expected greater and more exotic things from the secrets of the harem. I had to settle for seeing them hold their hair out over the burning *oudh* to scent it.

Kohl is used liberally around the eyes and I soon felt that my own looked colourless and unattractive. So I have begun applying my eye liner with a heavy hand. It doesn't improve my looks much but I don't feel so undressed. The shops are full of American and European cosmetics and the girls and their mothers experiment just as avidly as we.

One product you cannot get in Saudi Arabia is Revlon. I was told it is a Jewish company, but whether this is the sole reason or not I don't know. I do know that because of it there was a little incident here.

If the man at the customs desk had been more diligent when I went through he would have taken my one Revlon lipstick away from me, I am told. As it was I was able to keep it and am very happy, for I had searched some time at home to find one that was the exact mauve shade of my new dress. How many dabs of colour had I applied to my palm as I stood at the cosmetic counters in several department stores? I had, on one occasion, even worked up the side of my wrist, trying first one, then another. At last I found the perfect match. Without too much foresight I purchased but one. Unfortunately I discovered I cannot replace it here, so I am feverishly careful with it and it is worn *only* with that one dress! Can you imagine my dismay when I could not find it? I immediately announced its loss to everyone. Such is the tenor of my days that the disappearance of a lipstick takes on such grave importance! I was determined to find it! Lindy and I are the only people in the entire harem who have absolutely no privacy. Because there is so much pilfering here everyone keeps their bedroom doors locked at all times and carries their key with them. We do not have keys. Everyone, servants and family included, are in and out of our rooms. I suppose it is largely curiosity about us and our things. My bathroom is also convenient for the outside lawn area, and the girls sneak in here constantly to puff madly on a cigarette. I do not smoke, I hate the smell of smoke, but my little house reeks of it and sometimes when all three are in here consuming two or three fags in rapid succession, the air is a dense fog. Now they are terrified at the very thought that their father should find out they have ever had one puff on a cigarette, which is expressly forbidden. Yet here they feel free to smoke themselves into a quick case of emphysema because they figure everyone will think I am the heavy smoker. Does Jewaher really think I alone am responsible for that fog bank? Well, anyway, because everyone, for one reason or another, wants access to our quarters, we have been given no keys and I keep everything of value locked in my suitcase. This is extremely inconvenient, but my lingerie all but disappeared the first week I was here, for in spite of Lindy's warning, I had failed to keep everything locked up.

Knowing this, I was foolish to leave my lipstick conveniently displayed in the bathroom. It went the way of my comb, three pens, slips, nighties and peignoir, as well as several gifts I had received from Jewaher. I had given up hope of finding the lipstick with so many suspects, but one morning, low and behold, Nura appeared in the sitting room resplendent in a vivid gash of purple lipstick.

Throwing American diplomacy back twenty years, I exclaimed:

'Oh, Nura! You found my lipstick. How marvellous!'

'Is this yours?' she asked innocently. 'I'll go and get it for you right away.'

In a few minutes she was back with a worn-out, almost empty, very repulsive-looking pink lipstick.

'But that is not the colour you are wearing now, Nura,' I admonished in astonishment. I had been aware that the servants were light-fingered, but the princess? Flabbergasted is what I was!

'Lipstick turn this colour because I put on last night and it all worn off now,' she calmly explained.

I'm no Estée Lauder but I know freshly applied lipstick when I see it. Now what? I couldn't come right out and accuse her of lying. Even in America one doesn't do that. Her sister Fatima was present, however, and in a few minutes she took me aside.

'Nura have lipstick, okay, she have most everything we lose. I get.' Shortly afterward one of the maids was sent down to me with my long-lost lipstick in her hand. No reference was ever made to it again. Nura was as charmingly effervescent and friendly as ever. Now how about that? A little kleptomania in the royal closet?

Another example of this was the loss of my good pen. It had been a farewell gift from a couple of friends and was a real beauty. When I discovered it was missing I was not just annoyed, as I had been when the lipstick disappeared; I was heartsick at losing my beautiful memento of friendship. Again I had no idea where to look, so beyond announcing its loss, there was little I could do. Really, the whole subject of pens and pencils is an enigma I simple have not been able to figure out as yet. In the midst of all this wealth and opulence no one *ever* has a thing to write with. Whenever someone wants to take a message they shout for me to get my pencil; whenever they want to keep score for a game I must supply the lead. Whenever a paper must be signed I'm summoned to provide the pen. Whatever did they do in this huge place before I arrived? No one has anything to write with and no one would ever think to purchase something. It would be of little importance that I had to fetch and carry these items for the entire family, but they always have a most disconcerting habit of failing to return them. After several weeks of this bothersome state of affairs I began protesting. I have asked how they do their schoolwork, why they don't buy a few pens for themselves, what they did about messages before I came. All I ever get is a smile, a shrug of the shoulders, a shake of the head. After a while all of my own writing implements had gone, with the exception of the one pen I had received as a gift. Valuable both monetarily and sentimentally, I did not volunteer it for use by anyone, I needed a new supply! How simple if I were back home . . . just hop in the car, drive to the nearest stationer's and pick up whatever I want. But here, here it is enough to cause a nervous breakdown, or at the very least a case of the screaming meamies if I want something no one else is interested in at the moment. I knew three weeks of pleading, beseeching and begging lay ahead of me before someone would either take me to a store or direct one of the drivers to buy one for me. I began my drive:

'Jewaher, I need a pen.'

'Why?'

'I want to write to my family.'

'You no happy here?'

'Yes, of course, but they like to hear all about you. I need a pen in order to tell them how beautiful Saudi is, and how good you are to me.'

'Good, I will get.'

Flattery got me nowhere, for she promptly forgot all about it.

'Nura, I need a pen, I have no more, I cannot loan you any more. Can you remember to have your driver stop and buy one for me on your way from school?'

'Yes, I will get it for you today.'

'Nura, you won't forget will you?'

'Forget? I no forget, why you think this?' She forgot, she forgot everyday, she is still forgetting!

'Gada, all my pens and pencils are now gone, I cannot

help you the next time you want to take a message, please ask your driver to go today and buy me some.'

'I will tell him as soon as he returns with my new dress.' I knew that was a lost cause, Gada would never bother to remember something that did not directly benefit or interest her. If she didn't do it immediately, it wouldn't get done. I am still reminding her, she is still insisting she will get it for me shortly.

'Prince Faisal, how nice to see you, I have a problem I bet you can help me solve.'

'What is that, dear lady?'

'Well, you see, it's this matter of something to write with, I don't seem to be able to get hold of a pen or a pencil, can you suggest —'

'Say no more, I, Faisal, shall see that you have a fine pen right away. You must allow me to do this for you. I insist, it will be a gift from me to you, you must accept this little offering.'

The little 'offering' is still to be offered. The men are even worse than the women when it comes to forgetting their promises.

For two weeks I went around beseeching everyone I saw to help me. I was having no luck at all. Now this is an example of what I must go through for every single item I need or want. One instance is just a bit amusing, but after a while it wears you down, you find yourself dissolving in a puddle of tears because you have used the last of your toothpaste and you know what you will go through before you can get more.

With the loss of my good pen I was now deprived of my main source of personal activity, writing letters home. I felt frustration, and yes, a sense of despair at the loss and the knowledge of the difficulty I was having with getting another. But this time I was to be lucky.

Two days ago my maid ran into the house wildly waving something in her hand. My pen!

'Oh, oh, where ever did you find it?' I cried, hugging her ecstatically.

It seems she was walking back from the laundry room when

105

fifteen-year-old Prince Saud ran into her on his skateboard. As they picked themselves up she spotted my pen clipped to his *thope*. She simply told him it was mine and he handed it over without further ado. It is this strange lack of embarrassment that perplexes me. He knew I had been looking everywhere for my pen; he knew it meant a lot to me. When Marri saw it he did not try to deny that it was mine, but until then he was not about to volunteer to return it. When Nura knew that I was aware she had my lipstick, she was apparently not a bit disconcerted. Though she had tried to avoid returning it, she didn't spare a moment's blush when her sister retrieved it.

I notice that this 'talent' is extended to 'verbal inaccuracies' as well. In other words, they can tell the biggest whoppers, and when caught, they simply laugh as if it were a great joke and show not the slighest discomfort. This proclivity for lying, if you will pardon my bluntness, is something that is not restricted to either sex, or to any age. It seems to be a penchant of everyone here. How anyone can ever rely on another friend, relative, love or business associate, only God knows. Or rather, only Allah knows; I don't think God has this territory! Yet, in spite of this, they are so totally charming, so agreeable, so unabashed, you cannot take offence.

Another example of the daily frustrations that make life interesting here is the problem of the dry cleaners. Very shortly after I arrived I made such a mess of one of the good gowns that it had to be sent to the cleaners. Of course, not so long ago there was no such thing as a dry cleaner in all of Saudi Arabia, so I suppose I am extremely fortunate that there are many very fine ones here now. I gave that little thought, however, when I began finding that for me it was not a simple matter to have my dress either sent or picked up. What an exhausting experience it turned out to be.

A day or two after losing a bout with a particularly greasy hunk of lamb, I began requesting that my dress be sent to a cleaner. All amateur efforts at spot removal had failed and I feared for the future of my favourite gown. Well . . . would you believe it took twenty-four days of suggesting, requesting and finally shouting and madly waving the dress before it was given to Mohamet with instructions that he should take it to the new French cleaners? Secretly I feared the stains were by now so well set they would never be able to remove them, but at least it was on its way to a professional. After a suitable wait of about a week I then had to begin the hassle of trying to get it *back*. It practically caused an international incident as I became more and more upset. If these people had anything serious or important on their minds I could understand their total lack of concern for my desire to get the dress back, but it would only take them a moment to call the gate and have one of the drivers pick it up. Think I could implore anyone to do that? Not on your life; they simply couldn't understand why I was in such a tizzy over that dress. As a matter of fact I don't know myself; it is part of the mental erosion that the western mind goes through over here, I think. Such unimportant things take on monumental importance. Every day I began by asking everyone I met if they could arrange to have the dress picked up, or order a car for me so I could do it myself. The more I fussed the more they seemed to ignore me. Finally, almost in tears of frustration, I grabbed Gada's hand.

'It is my favourite dress, Gada; if we don't go for it soon they will lose it, it has been almost two months!'

'Why you no tell me before? I get right away,' she announced.

'Oh, Gada, I have told you, over and over, you never remember.'

'You never tell *me*; I, Gada get dress today!'

How could she forget so completely from yesterday? Did she really forget? Or did she simply not want to be bothered? Who knows, but this time I would not be put off. I pulled her to her feet and hurried her toward the door; she would not forget this time. I yanked her along to the gatehouse where the drivers were lolling around over their tea. It was bad timing . . . it was time for prayer soon, no point in going now, I was told. Defeated, I returned dejectedly to the sitting room.

A few days later I tried the same approach with Fatima. That time I got a little farther. Mohammed promised to pick it up on his way back from another errand. I waited as eagerly as if I were receiving a rare gift. Mohammed returned, I raced to the car. No dress. He had arrived there at six p.m., he said, but alas the cleaner closed at five!

It took several more days before I could stir anyone enough to make another effort. This time, they assured me, Hamdi would go and go early enough. When five o'clock came and went with still no dress I was told Hamdi had been unable to pick it up because only Mohammed knew which cleaners the dress had been taken to.

'Why didn't Hamdi ask Mohammed where it was?' Smiles and helpless shrugs were the answer to that question.

I was becoming quite paranoid about the whole thing. 'They just don't want me to have the dress,' I told myself, then, 'They don't care at all, they are selfish, self-centred, hateful!' Whatever they were, whatever they thought, you'd think they would help me to get the darned thing just to shut me up, I was becoming a terrible bore. Apparently that is what happened, for at long last Jewaher bestirred herself and sent Mohammed off at noon one day to retrieve the dress. At last, at last I was to have it, by now I almost didn't want it!

Mohammed reported in, *sans* dress. The machine at the cleaners had broken down. They were unable to clean it, it would be ready in two days. I stared at him in disbelief. They had had the dress just a day or two short of two months and had not been able to clean it? My credulity would not stretch that far. I still don't know what the true story was, why all the delays and procrastinations. I guess I never will know. Suffice it to say that two days later Mohammed walked in with the dress. The spots were gone. Jewaher smiled sweetly.

'Happy now?' she asked

Such was my sense of relief, mingled with the tension built of increasing frustration over the whole thing, I could barely choke out a grudging 'Shukran'.

I feel it is well past time for me to leave, but the thought of leaving Lindy and Tarek here alone is very upsetting, even if they do finally get around to securing my exit visa, which so far they have not. It seems to be as elusive as my dress . . . one vague excuse after another.

Love to you, and tell Bill I just finished 'Dynasty'; it is the last of the books he gave me to tuck in my suitcase. I thoroughly enjoyed it, for the feelings of the main character about the culture she had married into hit home with me here. I hated to see it end. Now Lindy is reading it.

Fondly,

Babs

Dear Aunt Helen,

I can hardly wait to tell you the funny sight I saw in town this evening! I had actually managed to get out for a trip to the Euro Marche, a huge sort of shopping mall where the more daring Arabian women are now having their drivers take them to enjoy the fun of shopping. As always, there was a carload of us: the three girls, two of the young princes and two servants, plus myself and the driver.

On the way home I sat up front next to the driver. This is the most coveted seat because not only are you uncrowded, so the driver will have room, but it is cool and you have an excellent vantage point. Suddenly we heard sirens and pulled to the side of the road. Three fire trucks passed us, sirens screaming as they roared along at about fifteen miles an hour. Everyone shouted with glee and excitement, exhorting Mohammed to follow the trucks. We fell in behind them, and slowly, ever so slowly, crept down the street. Now and then we turned a corner and proceeded a few blocks. I glanced back. A rapidly lengthening line of cars was streaming out behind us like the tail on a kite. It seemed we were going to a funeral, not a fire, from the speed at which we ambled along. I soon realised that we had circled the same block or two several times. 'Good Lord,' I thought, 'they can't find it!' We drove around in this aimless fashion for about forty minutes, the tail of our kite growing ever longer. At one point the leading engine drove down a dead-end street. It turned around, the other two trucks turned around, we turned around, and one by one all the long line of cars turned around and drove back out!

At long last, we could see a little knot of men and children standing around on a corner. They waved us on down the street to what appeared to be a large vacant lot with a high wall around it. Smoke billowed from the interior. Leaving royal dignity safely in the car, we all leapt out and clambered, in our long skirts, veils and high heels, up the embankment surrounding the wall. Inside we saw the gutted remains of a building, the flames long since gone. Only ashes, rubble and smoke remained. So much for the efficiency of the Saudi Fire Department.

In fairness to the Fire Department, I should point out that it is the Arab love of privacy and the lack of a home mail delivery that is probably responsible. Since there is no mail route to the private home there is no need of an address. You can always describe to your friends the location of your home, so what matter if there is no street name or house number? As long as the men have a location where they can receive their mail that is all that is necessary. The businesses, of course, do have addresses.

The men either don't want their women and children to receive mail that doesn't go to them first, or they simply don't consider it important enough to bother doing anything about it. I imagine some feel one way and some another. Also, if you can't read, what do you need mail for?

Actually, the lack of organised street and house identification has led to a very colourful practice in the foreign and Bedouin sections of town. The names of the people living there are written in bright paint on the walls by the entrance gates. The gates themselves are fascinating, for they are made of a solid metal that appears to be iron and are painted and decorated in a profusion of colour and detail. Then the names of the occupants are scrawled around it in reds, blues and greens, making the entire sight most picturesque.

Can you imagine how this casual approach to life would complicate things for you in the real estate business? When we go to call on someone who has invited us to see their new home, or to visit someone for the first time, we get to the general vicinity and then begin what seems like aimless wandering around, trying to locate the place from a verbal description. Sometimes we just give up and go home!

I imagine that you are having marvellous weather in beautiful La Jolla just now, I'm still looking forward to spending the Christmas holidays with you and all of the wonderful people there. In this barren land of sand I am more aware than ever of the enticing charm of your 'Jewel by the Sea', with its glorious climate, lush green vegetation, sparkling ocean and exotic flowers, to say nothing of its plentiful supply of conversation.

The Arabs may have a surplus cash flow of $315 million per day, but there is no place like home. My first stop will be Aunt Joie's lovely eyrie high on Hummingbird Hill in Reading, Pennsylvania. There, in early December, I hope to see some *snow*. After a good dousing in cold weather I shall be ready for the sun-drenched land of southern California.

Here in Arabia they tell me that October finds the weather cooling off somewhat from the incredible 120° to 130° of the summer. I understand that in winter it will actually get very, very cold, but no matter what the weather does, it does it in miles and miles and miles of nothing.

Another thing I definitely look forward to is a good old American cocktail party. Ye Gads, I've had my caustic say about their inanities in the past, but wash my mouth with soap! Never again will I turn up my nose at them. Every trite, banal remark uttered by a sweet young thing, every *sotto voce* comment by an errant husband, every hackneyed attempt at erudite wit by pseudo-intellectuals will have my happy, enthusiastic attention.

When I return I will scintillate and sparkle, yea, I will shower the multitudes with platitudes and truisms, and every insipid cliché by a 'callow youth' will be 'music to my ears'.

What brought on this outburst? You may well ask! Just attend one rousing party in Saudia and you will never question more. To attend one party here is a cultural experience. To attend two is interesting; to attend more is to subject yourself to agony worse than a size five shoe on a size six foot!

I have tried to analyse what it is about these catatonic conclaves that inspires such excitement and preparation. The answer eludes me unless, once again, it is simply the enjoyment of preparation, having a reason for fussing over another new gown, selecting the appropriate jewels, experimenting with a new hair-do. The parties are all alike, and all dismally dull and boring once you have seen the colourful array of fashion displayed by the young princesses.

Recently we attended a huge affair given to show off the

new home presented by a certain high-ranking prince to his latest bride. (He has had over thirty of them, bless his loyal little heart!) The home was beautiful, the young bride even more so. We arrived rather late, as always, and ascended the marble steps to the women's door. We were met by two elegantly gowned Nubian girls with incense. After being well-smoked (I always feel rather like a piece of salmon when they hold that incense beneath my skirts until it billows out around my ears) we proceeded to a huge sitting room ringed with the customary cushions. At one end of the room sat our hostess, dressed in a diaphanous gown of chiffon, its colours blending sea green, emerald, aquamarine and vibrant shades of blue. The deepest blue was at the low-cut neck which showed off a gorgeous cleavage that paled to insignificance beneath the most incredible diamond necklace I have ever seen. Four rows of perfectly cut stones converged to form a diamond bow at the back. Each stone appeared to be at least a carat, the ones at the ends of the bow graduating to half that size again. The matching earrings, bracelets and rings were equally breathtaking. The prince had indeed made a sizeable dent in the government's daily oil proceeds to purchase that little set of baubles.

After circling the room to kiss and be kissed we seated ourselves and settled back to take in the gowns and jewels of the rest of the assemblage, and to be looked over by them in turn. Our coffee and tea were served by a particularly voluptuous looking young girl who stood regally erect in the centre of the room throughout the evening, the graceful pot of ghawa in her apparently tireless hand.

We sat. No one spoke. The minutes dragged by. A half hour turned into an hour. We continued to sit and stare into space, trying to take in all the details of material, accessories and so on without actually looking. As the hour slowly crept towards two hours I fought the desire to leap up and say, 'Okay, everybody, let's all join in a rousing chorus of "Hail, Hail, the Gang's All Here".' I had to suppress a case of nervous giggles. I conquered the longing simply to rise and stretch. I was bored out of my mind as usual, and sank into a private reverie as I daintily sipped my tea and contemplated my fingernails, my toes, the hem of my skirt, the pattern of gold on the little cup. A funeral is livelier.

After about two hours of this merriment the hostess rose and left the room. We continued to sit and contemplate the carpet. Finally she returned, this time clad in a gorgeous taffeta confection of brilliant cerise that brought her dark beauty into full focus. Her appearance heralded the serving of the feast. We all rose and followed her to the garden where long linen cloths had been set out, laden with every conceivable delicacy.

About a hundred women sat down to eat. No one spoke. Occasionally a discreet whisper would be heard asking for a special dish to be passed. One of the things that astonishes me at these feasts is the way the servants walk up and down on the cloth to serve the larger platters. They weave amid the confusion of plates and bowls and trays, bare footed and with long skirts aswirl. I never caught one trailing their skirts through the *babaganoush, garson, moussaka* or *jareesh*. The mouth-wateringly delicious-looking cakes and pastries remained inviolate. How do they do it? The same way they pour that darn coffee into those thimble-sized cups in an eighteen-inch-long stream, I guess. Black magic!

Once again our hostess rises and leaves the garden. We follow suit, proceeding to the wash rooms to rinse our hands and have them dried and perfumed. Then we take a tour of the house. We see the various sitting rooms, the dining rooms, baths and games rooms. We see the lovely pool and sauna. Then we mount the stairs and view the huge room of the bride, her sitting room, luxurious bath and dressing rooms. They are opulent and fitted with western furniture throughout. Only the gorgeous carpets are oriental. Next comes the quarters of the groom. His apartments look like my mental image of a Playboy play room. Enormous, lots of furry rugs and carpets, a big bed that stretches from here to eternity on a dais at the far end of the room. Along one wall is a huge television set and every conceivable stereophonic gadget invented to date. I hope there are no more inventions to come, for there simply is no more room; they would have to move out.

At the conclusion of the tour we returned to the main salon to find the bride back in her seat, clad in yet another gown. I gasped in admiration. The past two gorgeous creations were as nothing beside this magnificence. Lush, lemon-yellow velvet was set off by exquisite coffee-coloured lace at the wrist and in a Queen Anne collar standing up to frame her face and neck. Her hair had been piled high and caught with a spray of topaz and diamonds. A huge topaz lay on her bosom, surrounded by diamonds in a delicate gold setting. It was worth the hours of sitting to view this dazzling creature. All Saudi parties do not boast this fabulous finish. She was exquisite.

Well, the so-called 'parties' are dismal, and, my dear, you have to take them on dead sober. At home anyone about to be subjected to such a thing would undoubtedly have a good stiff belt before hand, or at least a ladylike 'dressing drink'. Right?

You would think, with all this attention to personal appearance that I keep talking about, that the women must be inordinately vain, but they do not seem to be at all. Indeed, it is the men who display this quality in overwhelming abundance. It is the men who cannot bear to see a camera without begging you to take their picture. It is the man who struts and swaggers and constantly combs his hair, the man who cannot pass a mirror without admiring himself.

Every male is so eager to have his picture taken that I simply have to 'pretend' to snap them or I would never be able to provide all the necessary film. On the street they can spot a camera a block away and pose unabashedly. At home the young princes have to be ignored if I am to get anything other than their faces shoved in front of the lens. Then they badger me for days to see the finished products.

The women, on the other hand, are extremely shy and coy. Some will not allow pictures to be taken unless they are fully veiled. The young princesses are relaxed, and pose willingly when asked, but are much more interested in having me photograph the places and sites of interest. They do not like me to photograph anything they feel will show their country in a bad light, such as a lot of wrecked cars, or 'Chop Square', where hands and feet are lopped off once a week.

You know, I really did want that picture of the wrecked cars. I have heard stories in America of how when a Saudi prince wrecks his car he just leaves it there and buys another. In a sense that is true. When they hire their chauffeurs they insist on having excellent drivers, cautious, quick, intelligent. But they do not hold these characteristics essential for themselves. They all drive as if they had a death wish. To see them cut in and out of heavy traffic at top speed is terrifying. They swerve down the wrong side of the road, yell, shout and harangue each other. Out of town it is even worse. Here they push their high-powered latest-model cars to the limit and roar down the highways. They roar down the one-lane desert roads as well. Head-on collisions are an everyday happening and nobody walks away! In the rare event that the accident is not fatal, the car will still be so badly mangled that the only thing to do is leave it there to be carted off to the dump; then they do indeed need a new one.

Whenever we drive out of town I see several of these cars, smashed beyond any semblance of an automobile, lying along the road. The lots where these tangled bits of metal are taken contain piles that resemble small hills. Just car upon car upon car.

Naturally, the king and his brothers are upset about the seriousness of the situation, but until recently driving laws were apparently not very effective. Within the past two years I understand there has been a decided improvement, and hopefully before too long they will get the situation under control. Since I have been here a driver's licence has become mandatory. Prior to this anyone able to reach the pedals could drive. Now they must be of age and must have a licence. Of course, I noticed that the two young princes here simply sent their servants down with their pictures in order to get them. There doesn't seem to be a need for a prince to take a test. That is unfortunate for they are the main cause of the accidents. With their unlimited supply of pocket money they are easily able to purchase liquor at the exorbitant black-market rates, and like the American Indian, they have little tolerance for it. Liquor and fast cars have ever been a sorry combination. In addition to this, the police are loath to stop a prince for more often than not it will be the policeman who gets into trouble.

I heard of one prince recently who was arrested and jailed for drunken driving. He was so intoxicated he couldn't even identify himself. The next day when they discovered they had thrown a prince in jail they couldn't get rid of him fast enough. With many apologies he was released, while the poor fellow who arrested him lost his job. Of course, this is a second-hand story and as the young princes are sometimes known to brag a bit, as well as embroider the truth magnificently, the tale may not be accurate. But it probably is.

In another instance, for example, I saw a young man of the royal family initiate a real brawl on the street because he thought a passer-by had stared at his sister. The fight was broken up, but everyone assured me that had the police arrived it would not have been the prince who would be arrested for disturbing the peace. They had meant to allay my fears, but the injustice infuriated me. Had the police arrived, the poor fellow who had simply given a casual glance in the direction of a veiled woman could have been in serious trouble, and that rowdy who started it all would self-righteously walk away!

For the rest of the people, punishment is severe. Two of our cooks were involved in a fight last week in town and each was sentenced to eight days in jail and eight lashes on each of the eight days. Only the interference of Prince Abduraman saved them, and it was touch and go for a while as to whether he would involve himself or not.

Adduraman is a strange man. Infinitely polite and kind to me, he is also very reserved, quiet and shy. His life seems to be duller even than that of his wives and children. He rises each morning at 3:00 a.m. and calls all the men in his household to prayer, then takes care of business matters by phone. He has a non-royal, but extremely wealthy, business partner who actually runs the family business. There is considerable talk about the fact that this man robs the family of huge sums of money every year, but Abduraman will do nothing about it. This attitude toward theft is consistent with that of his wife, Jewaher, in her dealings with her light-fingered servants and children. She told me one day it would 'shame her' to make them lose face.

Abduraman never goes to the office himself, he seems to spend most of his time right here from what I can tell, with a few excursions to the ranch, which he loves, and for good reason.

At about nine o'clock he returns to spend several hours with whichever wife he had passed the night before. He sits beside her in the sitting room but doesn't talk. He reads the paper and tears out articles. Every time he sees the name of Allah he tears it out and saves it. By noon the paper is in shreds and he has a pile of torn-out pieces on the floor beside him.

During the morning hours he spends with Jewaher we usually absent ourselves, mainly by sleeping late, so they may be alone. I didn't understand this protocol in the early days of my visit and sat uncomfortable through a few of these quiet tête-à-têtes, Jewaher and I silently sipping our coffee, Abduraman reading and tearing. Promptly at noon he gathers up his articles and the mutilated remains of the paper and prepares to leave. Then Jewaher, who has sat contentedly mute until now, suddenly turns coy and tries to make him remain a little longer. They tussle and giggle together and obviously both enjoy the routine immensely. It ends by him remaining another five minutes, taking an extra cup of tea. Then he rises and walks slowly in his oh-so-dignified tread, out of the door, out of the building, and across the courtyard toward his own home where I can only suppose he has further prayer and his noon meal with the men of the household and guests.

About three o'clock each afternoon he arrives in the court-yard of the wife he will favour that night, happily fortified with another paper. After he has been ceremoniously greeted by all present, he will retire behind the protective barricade of his newspaper and remain there perusing and tearing away until once again the paper is in shreds and his allotted time has been spent. He gathers up all the pieces and strides off once more toward his own house, not to be seen by his womenfolk again until late evening. In the evening he sometimes has a paper, but more often than not will simply stare at the television.

The lives of all Saudi princes are not quite so dull or regimented, but I'm told this is it for a vast number.

The westernised princes take a more active role in their business affairs from what I can tell, though they all have people who actually run the day-to-day activities. They also spend much time out of the country. They have homes in London, and in the cities of Spain, Switzerland and America mainly. They enjoy spending time at these homes where their life-style is not dictated by their religion. When in Saudi, however, they follow the ways of their fathers quite closely and much time is spent visiting. They visit their sisters, aunts and mothers regularly, as well as the homes of their many men friends and relatives.

It is fortunate that they do this, for the presence of the male relatives adds some sparkle to the otherwise dull day of the womenfolk. Even with their company, conversation is still desultory and the main diversion is drinking tea and coffee. They do tease, however, and everyone loves the light-hearted banter that takes place.

Generally when a man is present at meal-time a huge repast is ordered for him by Jewaher and he eats it in the sitting room while we are there. He does not join the women in the dining area. I always feel this is surely embarrassing – to be the only person eating in a room full of people – but it is their way and doesn't bother them at all. Men are not expected to eat with the women. There have been two exceptions to this procedure since I have been here and both were highly exciting for the family.

The first of these occurred when they entertained the first-born son of one of Abduraman's other wives. He is your usual princely type, about twenty-five years old, quite handome, I'm told, meticulously polite, and incredibly imperious. What makes him a little more important than the other boys in the family is the fact that his mother is the daughter of the king, rather than just another prince. The women seem to be in awe of all men, from the religious training that men are naturally superiors. But they showed even greater awe of this young man because of his position. Apparently his visits to the quarters of his half-brothers and sisters are rare; he certainly hasn't put in another appearance since I have been here. So when it was known he would be here on a given date you might say the place went wild. Everyone had to have a very special gown to wear, and great attention was given to planning the feast. Special goats and lambs, the plumpest chickens and a truckload of fresh fruits and vegetables were brought in from the farm, and the cooks were in a tizzy of preparation. Every servant was given additional chores. Jewaher sent for special *oudh* and special spices; perfumers were filled with the most fragrant scents, after much sniffing and sampling of the many vials the gypsy woman brought. Much thought was given as to where the feast would take place. Finally it was decided that it would be in the main dining room. That is the one with twenty white velvet chairs around the long glass table. At last all was ready. The night finally arrived, and along with it, the legendary prince. I was not to have the honour of making his acquaintance, for by bad luck and/or bad management Lindy and I had another engagement that night and were not home for the evening. Yes, I managed to miss the one really big feast Jewaher gave while I was there, because we had a previous engagement we didn't want to break.

When we returned home about midnight the prince was gone but everyone was in a state of high euphoria. They rushed to greet us and began telling of the marvellous feast and the equally marvellous prince. I must get my camera and take pictures of the remains of the repast, quickly, before the servants took it all away. I rushed for the camera and then up to the dining room in Jewaher's home. What I saw astonished me. I should have known, I suppose, but I was not prepared for it . . . all that plush dining room furniture had been carried away and the banquet was spread out on a long cloth which lay on the floor as always!

On the cloth lay the remains of a truly enormous meal. Beautiful it must have been when originally set down, for

120

even at this stage, dried out, melted, cold, and two-thirds devoured, it was an awesome culinary display. Potatoes, rice and pastas had been prepared in every conceivable manner. Chicken bones, lamb and goat carcasses, camel and beef were recognisable; huge platters of exotic *hors d'oeuvres*, desserts of every kind, silver bowls once laden with fruits, and dozens of unfamiliar dishes greeted my eye. It was indeed a feast the likes of which I will probably never see again. And I missed it. Isn't that like me?

The next special event that involved everyone eating together was one evening when the favourite uncle arrived to visit. He is also my favourite man, handsome, charming and totally westernised in his ability to talk in relaxed and excellent English. We sat around in the upper courtyard, which is also my favourite place, being romantically oriental in atmosphere, and as we sat talking Abdullaziz surprised everyone by pulling out a menu from a new Chinese restaurant. What excitement that created can only be appreciated if you remind yourself that most of the women present, and some of the young men, had never been in a restaurant in their lives! Abdullaziz suggested that we send out for a feast, further suggesting that since none of them were familiar with Chinese food, Lindy and I should make the selections. He was also considerate enough to recommend that we consider three or four hundred dollars as a fair amount to spend. We ordered a sumptuous meal, for there was a small gathering that night of only about a dozen people. The driver was duly despatched to bring the food back and everyone settled down to wait. It is a good thing that I am learning the Arabic disregard for time, because it was almost three hours before the drivers showed up with all the cartons and boxes and trays of food.

Ah, but it was worth the wait; it was absolutely delicious and everyone had a sensational time. The restaurant had sent along everything and so there we all sat, cross-legged on our Arabian carpets, merrily downing our meal with chopsticks. There was much laughter and for once I spilled less than anyone else, a fact that did not go unnoticed. It was an evening to remember for everyone.

And now, dear one, the time has come for me to bring this to a close. I have not received any mail in all these many, many weeks so I am beginning to believe I shall not, but I'll continue to write for I know it is no one's fault. I'm sure it will not be long before I get my exit visa and begin my slow but exciting journey home through Egypt, Greece, Rome and Spain. I have not been to Egypt before, although all my life it has been a place I have longed to see. Did you know that when I was about seventeen I wanted to be an Egyptologist? Maybe I confided that to you way back then. At any rate I changed my mind somewhat precipitately when someone pointed out that the tombs were full of poisonous snakes.

Aloha, darling Aunt, say hello to everyone for me and I'll see you in December, *Ensh Allah*!

Love,

Babs

Dear Aunt Joie,

Jewaher is so kind and generous to me that I really feel ungrateful when I think how eager I am beginning to be about the thought of leaving here. Hopefully it will not be too long. How I want to see Lindy and the baby leave at the same time! I'm anxious to see Europe again and then head for friends and family in that wonderful Mecca of the emancipated female, the U.S.A.

If I knew exactly how long I am still to be here, I'm sure I would relax and enjoy every minute, but the not knowing, the nagging little fear that it could be a long, long time, makes me somewhat itchy to be on my way. I queried again the other day about the state of my elusive visa . . . now they tell me I must have a photograph taken before anything further can be done and since the weekend is coming up there isn't any point in doing anything about it now.

Well, the weeekend is over, but they inform me that Yosseph has taken his family to Jedda for a short vacation, so there is no need for a photograph anyway right now. There is always some perfectly reasonable excuse, yet it only took one day to handle the entire matter when Jewaher was ready to send one of her servants back to Egypt! If only I were able to do something about it myself, such as go to the visa office and stand in a mile-long line just to be told it would take a month – anything would be better than just sitting here listening to one excuse after another, not able to do a thing but accept them.

Another problem I am having, which is probably trivial but which seems to have become monumental in my eyes lately, is the matter of learning the Arabic language. It is *not* easy! When I arrived I could say hello, goodbye, thank you, please, and a few other little phrases – fifty words in all. Now three months later, I am only at about 500 words and nearly all of those are nouns.

Almost from the day I arrived I began asking for a

dictionary and a book or two on Arabic, so that I could study the grammar. One of the difficult things is that the words for speaking to a female are different from those used in speaking to a male. Even if the word itself is not different, it has a different ending. So it's much more complex than Spanish or French. I had as much luck procuring any books as I have had getting anything else. Lots of promises but no action.

I had learned my basic fifty words from a little travel guide to Egypt, and naturally, although it never occurred to me at the time, it was all geared for the male traveller. There wasn't a note to tell you that you don't address a woman in the same way as a man, so I dutifully learned the words and went off armed with a small list of amenities about which I must say I felt totally smug. Imagine being able to say, *'Moya, min fudluck,'* or *'Wein foonduck?'* Or more importantly, *'Wein beit moya?'* (Water, please – Where is the hotel? – Where is the bathroom?) Obviously I had reason to be ecstatic about my prowess as a linguist. Until I arrived here! The first week I had asked for so many glasses of water, just to get in the conversation, that I was practically afloat, but I had no use at all for 'where is the bathroom?' as they had shown me exactly where it was almost immediately after my arrival. As for the hotel, I keep trying to work it into the conversation but it isn't easy: if you can't go there, who cares?

Once again the good manners of the Arabian people have stood in the way of progress as far as my linguistic endeavours are concerned, for when I make a blooper, which I must do nearly every time I open my mouth, everyone is much too polite to correct me. It took weeks before I learned that I had been speaking the words of my little guide book inappropriately to the women. Thank goodness the children, although also very polite to me, are not yet as adept at controlling their facial expressions. One day I asked a servant to get me something and saw a quick surprised smile flash across the face of the fifteen-year-old Saud.

'What have I said?' I asked him.

'You say 'man words' to woman, words good, but not good for her.'

I was dumbfounded! Saud, of whom I am particularly fond,

speaks about the same amount of English as I do Arabic, so we had considerable trouble establishing what I was doing wrong. At last I understood that there seemed to be almost two different languages for the two sexes. Mostly it turned out to be the addition of feminine endings on words, but the endings seemed to change, and I didn't know what he meant by different beginnings. I still don't know exactly which words change, and it appears in some instances the words change completely.

It really is most complex and without any books on basic grammar I just cannot figure it out sufficiently to make much progress. Lindy has just given up trying and takes no interest at all. 'Bess,' for example, which means 'enough', is the same for everybody, while the word for 'good' changes from 'kways' to 'kwaysa' when used in speaking to a woman. Well, can you believe I have been running around here talking to all these women for weeks as if they were men and no one told me I was doing it wrong?

The words from my booklet and the words I have learned here are a real jumble! I renewed my efforts to get a book on Arabic. With all the Americans working here for Aramco I know such books must exist. All the people who speak English here say to me, as they did to Lindy, 'You must learn to speak Arabic.' Well, thanks a lot! What do they think I have been trying to do? They always say they learned English by just listening and talking to people. They seem to forget completely that they had plenty of books to help and that when they were in America they took classes in English. They also talked a lot with Americans, and it was a combination of the two that enabled them to learn. They agree that they did take classes in English, but these weren't what taught them the language. I can't convince them that unless you are a linguist by nature, it sure helps to be able to look up a word you have heard in a book, or ask someone its meaning. Verbs are the rascals that are driving me crazy. I have a little notebook and everywhere I go the notebook goes with me. But when they are excited, which is most of the time, they all speak so rapidly that it's difficult for me to catch much of what is said. However, whenever I am able to make out a particular sound and its meaning I write it down in the book and add it to my vocabulary. My booklet looks like this:

shiklik – looks like (???)
goomee – stand up (check before learning)
koolookum – all of it
badain – later
floos – money
Bit rhuhee ilyom? – Are you going today? (Does 'bit' mean are?)

One day just after I thought I had deciphered the difference between the masculine and feminine for 'Do you speak', only to find I had interpreted it all wrong, and then discovered that 'I don't know' was either 'Anna baruf,' or 'Anna barafish', or 'Ma adri,' but I couldn't figure out which, a small tear of frustration trickled down my cheek.

Jewaher spotted it immediately.

'Enti hazeen?' she asked. Was I sad?

How could I explain the frustration I was feeling, wrestling daily to learn a language that seemed to elude me at every word? I struggled to tell her the trouble I was having, and how much I wanted an English/Arabic dictionary.

'Nam, Ma atkelumin Araby zein.' I hoped I had said, in the feminine, that I could not learn to speak Arabic well.

She couldn't bear to see me unhappy, but the simple solution of granting my request for a book never occurred to her. She spoke to her servant, who left the room and returned a few moments later with a length of gorgeous green satin sari cloth, heavily embroidered with gold and cerise thread. It was exquisite.

'Kwaysa?' she asked. Was I happy now?

How was I to tell this dear woman that it was not 'goom-aszh hellowa' (beautiful material) that I wanted, when to her it was an infinitely more desirable gift than a silly book?

'Anna mabsut,' I smiled, hoping I had said that I was happy.

One day my ineptitude with the language brought an entirely different reaction from my hostess. We were having visitors of some importance and Jewaher had ordered the cooks to go to particular pains with the meal. She had made a special trip to the kitchens to oversee some of the preparations. Wanting to say something complimentary about the meal I knew was forthcoming, I asked Khalid, who happened to be watching television in the room at the time, how to say 'excellent meal'. Armed with my newest little sentence I went in to dinner along with all the guests, happy that I could offer some pleasantry.

The meal was really very well done, with several new dishes, and everything displayed on the platters to look just beautiful and 'much too good to eat', as the saying goes. I felt my phrase would be most appropriate.

'Hadthi akil jamel,' I announced in a clear voice.

Instead of the look of pleasure I expected to see on Jewaher's round face, I saw her draw herself up, turn very red, and tighten her mouth! I saw the shocked faces of the guests.

What in the world had I said?

Again Saud was the one to enlighten me.

'You tell her this is camel food,' he whispered in my ear.

Khalid had not been above having a little joke at my expense. I was furious till I realised that it wasn't so very far from something any teenaged American boy might enjoy doing. Really it *was* funny, if only it hadn't embarrassed poor Jewaher in front of her guests.

There is a problem, too, with the spelling translation from Arabic to English. It is every man for himself, as no one appears to care how to spell words correctly in English at all. I wanted to know how to spell the name Mischaelle and came up with four or five variations. It didn't matter which I used, according to them, whichever I liked would be fine. Some of them liked Michaelle, others Mischaelle and some Mischalle. I guess when you try to take a word that has always been written in Arabic and put it into our alphabetical system that is bound to happen. It accounts for the fact that when you read several different accounts of Saudi Arabia there will be that many different ways of spelling the various words. *Souk, suq* and *suque* all mean the marketplace, for example. A bit confusing, but phonetically it is understandable, which is what counts, I suppose.

From the amount of fussing I have been doing in this letter you would swear I am utterly miserable. Actually nothing could be farther from the truth. I'm having an absolutely marvellous time. Considering the fact that all we really do is sit on the floor and sip tea, it is amazing how much goes on around here.

Every now and then the ghastly thought crosses my mind that I must be gaining weight at a horrifying rate. How will I ever get into my western clothes when I get home? I have not located a scale to find out the bitter truth, but I know it is happening. Inevitable. I am not so distressed that I am willing to forego the midday meal or begin a serious exercise regime, though. It is indeed a lazy existence.

And the weather! Aunt Joie, you know how I grumble about the rain – I have been here going on four months now and not one drop of the stuff have I seen. And would you believe I don't miss it a bit? It would be fun to see snow, however, when I get home. Do order snow for me, dear Aunt Joie.

Tarek grows cuter every day. He is fifteen months old, but is very tall for his age, and straight. He seems extremely alert and most precocious with anything mechanical, but he doesn't say as many words as my girls did at that age. He is certainly in grave danger of being irreparably spoiled with all the constant attention he receives. He never cries; why should he? Everything is his immediately.

I do miss getting mail from home. For some reason I thought I would be deluged with letters from friends and family. I didn't count on the Saudi mail service – or maybe it's the American service? At any rate, all this time and not a note. I am so hungry for news of everyone, also news of the international scene. *What* is going on out there?

Bushels of love dear one,

Babs

Dear Pat,

Perhaps it will not come as a surprise to you that Lindy's marriage to the prince seems unable to survive the stress of their cultural differences. It is sad to see two young people still so much in love unable to bridge the tremendous gap that separates them. But nothing in the life of an American girlhood can ever prepare a person for the role of a Saudi wife.

Lindy has tried for two years, but cannot make the adjustment. She has finally asked Abdul Raman to let her return to America with me and he has agreed. According to their customs the father may allow the mother to keep her children under the age of ten, so my grandson will come to stay in America also, and for this I am very grateful. For Jewaher it is devastating.

Only last night I heard an oral expression of all the many heartaches Jewaher has been enduring. They caused such shame and despondency that they finally culminated in her attempt at suicide. She has been bearing the burden of Fatima's unhappiness and rebellion, Gada's apparently hopeless love and spinsterhood, and the drinking, smoking and reckless driving of her older sons. Then, added to all this, came the realisation that she may never know the joy (so terribly important to a Saudi woman) of bringing up her first grandson. It is always painful and sad for grandparents to lose contact with beloved grandchildren through divorce or separation, but for a Saudi family it is particularly tragic.

Usually, when a marriage breaks up here the children of the union are at least still in Arabia! In this case he will be on another continent, separated by other lands, seas and huge oceans. It overwhelmed her, and as she contemplated it all she reached for the pills that would bring her peace.

The sudden encroachment of western ways on the lives of these unsophisticated people is bringing so much misery and turmoil to many families. My own relief and joy that *my* grandson will be brought up in America is tinged with guilt.

One does not like to experience these emotions at the expense of another's pain. Such is the ripple effect of the complications arising from marriages between people of such differing backgrounds. It appears that the old saying, 'Never the twain shall meet,' has proved true once again.

My daughter is *very* lucky! I wonder how many young girls considering marriage with an apparently westernised Saudi are really aware of what they may get into? I would say none of them. When American girls marry Arabian boys they find a whole new world, exciting and also devastating. For example, he may divorce her if he desires, but she may not divorce him at all unless he agrees to it, and since he may take another wife at any time, he may well just up and dump her at his mother's home and forget her. She cannot go to the American embassy and expect help, for when she enters Arabia she does so as a Saudi wife and gives up her right to expect help from the United States. Our government will not jeopardise Saudi-American relationships for the sake of one unhappy girl. She cannot escape. If she leaves the harem or her home and attempts to get around the town or city alone she risks being picked up by the M'Tawas. If she should get to an airport she cannot board a plane without an exit visa, and you know already the trouble involved with trying to get one of those! No, once in you had better be prepared to stay whether things work out or not.

I have talked to a number of European and American wives, and not one of them has expressed happiness in their marriage. They all say their husbands became totally different people once they returned to Arabia, and the great wealth some of them have does not compensate for the life they must lead when here in this country.

Prince Saleh's pretty young wife, fabulously rich though she now is, and free to spend half the year at her homes in England or Spain, says that were she to refuse to return to Arabia or try to leave her husband, she would most certainly lose her sons. Raised as princes of Saudia, they would never give up their life there to live abroad permanently, even if their father would allow it. Her sons are ten and twelve.

Isn't it sad, the unhappiness and actual danger our hearts

lead us into when we are young and fall in love? Every girl who is remotely contemplating such a marriage should read the Koran. Read it from beginning to end, with the realisation that the men of Islam truly believe every word that is written, incredible as that may seem to a western mind. No matter where they were educated, or how Europeanised or American-ised they may seem, their faith is a deeply-rooted part of them in a way most of us cannot identify with, and their convictions and values are all based on it.

For example, it is vital to know and understand that accor-ding to the Koran men have authority over women because Allah has made the one superior to the other. Now, you didn't know that, did you? The women here believe it. In order to survive here a woman just about has to believe it. Imagine sharing your life with a man brought up on readings from his Holy Book which tell him that 'good women are obedient . . . as for those who are not, admonish them and send them to beds apart and beat them.' Yes, that's right, beat them.

And how do you like this one? 'Women are your fields: go, then, into your fields as you please.'

If that one affronts your sense of fair play, what about the religious law that states if a woman commits fornication she is to be confined to her house until death, while almost in the same breath comes the happy news that Allah has provided many women for the men because 'man was created weak, and Allah, being merciful, wishes to lighten his burden'.

Now as far as I'm concerned, if Allah actually said that, She sure wasn't thinking!

Then there is this charming piece of advice to the husband: 'Mothers shall give suck to their children for two whole years if the father wishes the sucking to be completed.' However, if the father wishes, it goes on to state that he may certainly hire a nurse instead, so long as he pays her adequately. Yes, it is indeed a man's world over here.

Have you by any chance read the Koran? It refers time and again to the Paradise that awaits the true believer:

'For those that fear the majesty of their Lord there are two gardens . . . planted with shady trees. . . . Each is watered by a flowing spring. Each bears every kind of fruit in pairs. . . .

They shall recline on couches lined with thick brocade, and within their reach will hang the fruit of both gardens. . . . They shall dwell with bashful virgins whom neither man nor *jinnee* will have touched before.

'Virgins as fair as corals and rubies . . . shall the reward of goodness be anything but good? . . . And beside these there shall be two other gardens of darkest green . . . A gushing fountain shall flow in each . . . Each planted with fruit-trees, the palm and the pomegranate. In each there shall be virgins chaste and fair . . . Dark-eyed virgins sheltered in their tents . . . They shall recline on green cushions and rich carpets . . . Blessed be the name of your Lord, the Lord of majesty and glory.'

With all these virgins running about I do not find anything that tells me what happens to the poor earthly wives when they get to Paradise, although I would venture to say they probably have a much better claim to the place than the men by virtue of the fact that it is mighty hard for a woman to do much sinning around here.

Oh, but I, with some small degree of innocence, aided and abetted Nura, Gada and Fatima in what may well be thought of as a most sinful act. I must tell you all about it.

We went to a public place and had dinner. Yes, we went to a hotel and ate! Not just once, but *three* times! It happened after I had been here long enough to be absolutely ready to climb the walls (and here you can take that literally) but not long enough to have a true understanding of the enormity of such a defiant act on the part of three Muslim girls. I did not know until much later that they told their mother they were going shopping. I was surprised to see that for this momentous occasion the girls had not bothered to dress up particularly. I had spent an hour getting ready!

The first night we spent a great deal of time driving around the city to minor hotels. At each one our driver would jump out, run inside for a few moments, return to the car and take off again.

Our communication skills were still pretty poor at this time but Lindy and I finally figured out that he was asking if they would allow five women to dine in their hotel restaurants.

The answer was no at the first five or six places but finally we were lucky. There was much fussing before we entered to be sure our veils completely covered us. Then we went in, our driver leading the way, with me trying to appear nonchalant when I felt like the witch of Endor, shrouded as I was in black cloth, and the girls timidly scuttling along at my heels.

The dining room had a desultory scattering of men at various tables around the room. I saw not a single woman. We followed the head waiter quickly, all of us wishing to be seated and out of the limelight. I felt my cheeks growing red as I saw every male eye upon us. Can you realise how silly this embarrassment was when I was covered from head to toe in veils?

I wasn't prepared for what happened next! We were ushered into a small room containing three or four tables and the door was firmly closed. We were to eat alone! I had been uncomfortable in the dining room with everyone watching us, but I wasn't ready to be shut up in a little room with no other people. If this was dining out Arab style we might as well have stayed at home.

The girls, however, were in seventh heaven, like girl scouts at a picnic. They went wild! They took off their veils, lit up their cigarettes, giggled and shrieked with delight. Even Lindy's usual dignity deserted her. Everything was hilariously funny. They ordered two bottles of ersatz wine and if I didn't know better, I'd swear they all got drunk! How could four females make so much noise? The food was mediocre Arab fare, but the service was excellent. When the meal was ended and the veils were all securely in place we ventured forth. Our driver had been patiently standing guard outside the door all that time.

Excited by the triumph of this foray into the outside world, the girls decided to try it again a few nights later. This time they cautioned me not to dress up too much and a glimmer of light began to flicker . . . was there something surreptitious about these outings? Did Jewaher know what was up? Weighed against the thought of not going out at all, I didn't have the strength of character to find out.

The last time I had bubbled with laughter as I compared our ride around town trying to find a second-rate hotel that would take us in, to a sailor with his one-night stand. This time, emboldened by the success of our previous adventure, Gada instructed Hamdi to drive us directly to the new Marriott Hotel. This time, too, we stepped out of the car and swept toward the entrance with due dignity, entering the sumptuous lobby with considerably more *élan* than we had displayed the last time. We even took a brief tour of the place, seeing the indoor fountains, prayer rooms, lounges and gift shops before we entered the dining room.

This was more like it! The dining room was crowded with beautiful people. Men and women of every nationality, the women expensively coiffed and gowned. I couldn't hide a sigh of pure pleasure. It was just like home! But what . . . where . . . ohh! I groaned as I saw what was to happen to *us*. Not for the veiled ladies of Arabia this glittering array of people enjoying the glamorous life of a fine hotel's dining salon. No, for us there was a small room with a closed door. A second time we were to dine alone!

Once again I watched the royal bearing of the girls vanish into the rapidly disappearing bottle of ersatz champagne. Their voices rose, their giggles were shrill, they chain-smoked through the entire meal. The cuisine was American and delicious. I had the lobster, but it was the first time I had seen steak and veal piccata eaten between puffs on a cigarette! Somehow it seemed sacrilegious. Salad, baked potato, onion rings, rolls and fresh strawberries completed our meal.

The service was good. What am I saying? The service was *too* good! The novelty of having three young Arabian women to serve attracted a bevy of waiters. They hovered over the little princesses like bees around a honey pot. We were never alone throughout the entire meal. When we were preparing to leave, the chef himself came to the table to present us with a special cake to take home, and as we approached the doorway from the main dining room to the lobby, seven waiters and the *maitre d'hôtel* lined up to say thank you for coming and request that we come back.

We must have made some sort of history that night. I can't

imagine any hotel actually wanting a repeat visit from these noisy silly hoydens, but apparently the hotel personnel viewed it as a break-through.

A week later we ventured forth again, this time to the Cutlery, but alas, I was feeling defiant. After all, I reasoned, I was not an Arab. Once inside the restaurant filled with European and American businessmen, their wives, and various Aramco personnel, I dropped my veil. Of all the bad luck! One of the many uncles was dining there and saw me enter the room! Of course he came over and spoke graciously to us, and I doubt he mentioned the incident to anyone, but it was our last night out in public.

I took quite a few good pictures of the girls in the restaurants each time, and of the interior of the Marriott Hotel, but I have none of them. The drivers have strict orders to take all finished pictures to Gada immediately. She goes through them and I receive only those safe for public viewing in her eyes. This is very frustrating, but since they provide the film and have them developed for me, I am not able to do more than wonder aloud where all the great shots are.

Well, Pat, time once again to call it a day. Say hello to everyone for me, won't you?

Love,

Babs

Hello Bill,

The days slip by and I grow lazier. I sometimes wonder how I ever lived the feverishly busy life I did, and ponder whether I shall be able to resume it when I return. I miss our Saturday afternoon coffees; we always found time for those, didn't we?

There is always something going on around here, though. Today's excitement was caused by a little lizard called *thatour*. The poor thing had the bad judgment to enter Fatima's bedroom. What a commotion it caused! When she spotted it she ran out screaming. The maid ran in, the maid ran out. Two of the boys ran in; the boys ran out. Four male servants arrived, armed with a variety of brooms, baskets, sticks and containers. They entered very cautiously. No big game hunter in darkest Africa ever approached his quarry with more care than that displayed by those four men as they crept up on the motionless little lizard. Suddenly, the lizard darted between their legs! With a shout, they tore for the door, bumping into one another, knocking each other down, as all scrambled to get out at the same time. Pandemonium! The crowd outside the door shrieked! The men screwed up their courage and approached the room again. Carefully they moved the huge wardrobe behind which the lizard was now hiding. Again it darted, this time up the wall. Again, at its movement, the men ran, yelling, from the room. After a time everyone calmed down enough to consider what to do next. Back they went to hit at the walls with the brooms, and predictably, the *thatour* raced down the wall to the floor where an excited Egyptian hurled a basket at it and, by sheer luck, succeeded in having it fall over the lizard. The yelling and leaping around subsided. Amazed at his good fortune and considerably braver now that the creature was out of sight, the servant stole forward and slipped a lid under the overturned basket, then with bated breath, he righted it. A whoop went up from the transfixed onlookers. Everyone began pounding the man on the back. He was a hero! That harmless little gecko wasn't over four inches long. The people here are terrified of them because they believe they are poisonous and if you touch them, or if you eat or drink anything they have touched, you will die.

The attitude toward animals in general is very different here. These children have no pets, which astonished me at first, as there are so many children! The place abounds, however, with cats! It reminds me of the Palatine Hill in Rome. Dozens and dozens of the mangiest looking cats and kittens you ever saw. I spotted one of these little kittens shortly after my arrival here; an emaciated little scrap of grey fur that had become separated from its mother and wandered down by my door. When I bent down to pick it up, its fur stood up, its back arched, and it began spitting furiously. Everyone shrieked warnings and Gada ran over, grabbing my outstretched hand.

'La, la,' (no, no) she exclaimed!

Her motions made it abundantly clear that this was no household pet but a wild animal. The glaring eyes, needle sharp claws and vicious-looking little teeth of the kitten itself left no doubt in my mind that it was not to be petted.

As time went on I came to realise that these cats are kept only to control the rats, mice and lizards. To be sure, they do their job. They are not fed and are kept in a wild state. Ferocious as they are, the children grow up knowing you will be badly hurt if you attempt to become familiar with them. Humans and felines give each other a wide berth.

Dogs are also objects of fear. I discovered this one day when a sociable setter from the Aramco compound, a few blocks away, came bounding in through our gate. It was a beautiful animal, high-spirited, friendly and delighted at having found a new place to explore and new people to charm.

The two guards at the gate let out a yell, hiked up their *thopes* around their knees, and lit out across the compound, the setter bounding genially after them. It was a ludicrous sight and I watched in amusement until I saw a third guard tear out of the guard house brandishing a long, stout stick. The dog sank down low on his front legs, his rear high and his tail waving in happy anticipation of the game ahead. He was ready to spring in any direction to fetch the tossed stick. I arrived, breathless, and threw myself at the dog, who acknowledged my presence with a polite slurp of his tongue across my cheek, but his body quivered with excited anticipation as he kept his eyes glued on the stick, awaiting the toss. The men, who had been shrieking and leaping about as if they were barefooted on a bed of live coals, hesitated when they saw me with my arms around the dog's neck. They backed away in a mixture of fright and good-natured embarrassment. I reached for the stick and lured the dog back outside the gate.

There the setter and I cavorted affably for ten minutes or so, while servants and family huddled behind the gate to watch. A brave Saud and his brother Hamud somewhat hesitantly joined me and I introduced them to my new friend. At first they were cautious, but soon began romping with obvious enjoyment, and swaggered back with considerable pleasure at their own audacity.

Each time we attempted to return to the gate the dog would come charging along after us, tail madly wagging, and everyone would scatter with shrieks of excitement and, by now, mock horror. Finally the boys and I managed to elude him and we dashed inside, the guards quickly slammed the gates shut. We collapsed in a heap of exhausted laughter while the more timorous plied the adventuresome boys with questions. It was a great day; much laughter and excitement tinged with the proper amount of chills and thrills for all of them.

I tried to explain how people in my country enjoy pets of all kinds. I talked about how you can tell a friendly animal from one that is ferocious or frightened, and how to approach one. I wanted them to realise you do not normally run up and throw your arms around the neck of any strange animal. They were intrigued, though I don't know how much they understood.

Shortly after that Musab decided to buy a bird. He and his servant came home laden with cage, seed, gravel, toys, feeding cups and of course the bird, a cute little budgie. Again everyone crowded around, stimulated by something new. For several days the bird was the centre of much curiosity, but then interest waned and soon it was forgotten. Unfortunately, it was forgotten by Musab as well, and one day the poor little thing was found dead in a cage devoid of all food and water.

My animal-loving daughter and I were devastated, but no one else seemed particularly disturbed. It reminded me of the day at the ranch when ten-year-old Abduraman came in with a tiny little wren he had shot with his new rifle. Jewaher popped the little thing into the coals which boiled the coffee. The feathers burned off as, with a stick, she turned it a time or two and then removed it. She tore its little body into tiny pieces and meted them out to the children clustered eagerly around. That day, too, I had been distressed to see a lovely little creature wantonly killed. It seemed quite barbaric to me as I watched them tear apart and devour the bird. But they probably think I am very strange for wanting to make pets of cats meant to catch mice, and birds meant to be eaten.

There are so many strange things to adjust to over here, I'm sure it must be equally confusing for the young people who are sent to America to go to school. For example, they must wonder why we take two or three cars to go somewhere, when everyone can just pile in to one car and be together.

Last night we were to do something very special! We were going to a carnival! The girls had only been allowed to go to one once before in their lives. This was a huge treat because I am here and special allowances were to be made. Well, eighteen of us crammed into the station wagon. In the front seat was the driver, one servant and myself in the seat of honour by the window. All the rest – three servants, the four girls, a little half-sister, and seven boys ranging in age from four to seventeen – piled in the back. We drove and drove, it seemed like forever in the heat and with all the noise of the excited crowd. Actually, it was about forty-five minutes. At last we could see the lights ahead, then the ferris wheel against the sky, and then the roller coaster. Excitement reached a fever pitch. The place was mobbed, cars everywhere. There was no organised parking and we wove our way through the bedlam. That we did so safely is a real testimonial to the skill of our Egyptian driver. At last we were parked and everyone tumbled out. The driver went off to reconnoitre and make arrangements for the family. In a few minutes he was back with the news. Ladies' Night had been cancelled. We could not go in! The boys, however, being under the age of eighteen, were able to go any night, as were the servants.

I was secretly less than delighted when I found that the boys would go in and we would sit in the car and wait for them. How long would it take seven boys to get their fill of such a wondrous festival? It was gruesomely hot, and in my long skirts and veils I was stifling. I settled down to a long period of self-pity. Apparently I was not the only one, for after about twenty minutes of this wretched ordeal, Gada suddenly gave orders to Hammet. The car started up, the air-conditioning was turned on, and with a sense of blessed relief, we drove out of the packed parking lot, down the highway and toward the lights of town. I could hardly believe my eyes! We pulled up in front of a sweet breath of home – an American-style ice-cream parlour! Not only that, we went inside and ordered our own ice cream! Always before when we stopped at any ice cream or *schwarma* stand, we had to give our order to the driver and sit, fully veiled, in the car until it was brought to us. There was never any opportunity to peruse the menu or ponder over choices. Here we stood in an agony of happy confusion, reading every word of every selection, deciding on this then switching to that, then back again.

It is not just because I was so thrilled to be there that I say the ice-cream parlours in Arabia are the best I have ever been in. All Saudi business establishments give a great deal more for your order than you would get at home. Here we could say, and be given, 'More nuts please,' 'Go very heavy on the cherries,' and 'I'd like a spoonful of caramel sauce on my hot fudge sundae, too.' We asked for doubles on *everything* and, believe me, our cups raneth over. At last we sat back, stuffed, sated, miserable and divinely content.

We drove back to the fair and though it took almost an hour to round up all seven boys and the servants, we didn't even mind. It was a memorable evening.

I mentioned *schwarma* and I don't believe I've told you

about this delicious snack. The open-air booths that sell these savoury Arabic sandwiches remind one of the stalls in Mexico. They are not exactly immaculate and there's no escaping a qualm or two about possible food poisoning, but once you have sunk your teeth into one of these succulent, spicy morsels, you will never again be able to resist them, and hang the consequences. You can have your choice of chicken, beef or lamb, which you see slowly turning on spits in the stall. If you are hungry the tantalising aromas and mouth-watering juices make a choice extremely difficult; all are delicious. The meat or chicken is carved from a roast in long slices; a piece of *pita* bread is spread with a variety of spicy concoctions; your selection is placed on it in piles of thin slices, followed by an assortment of items that might include such strange but toothsome additions as mashed potatoes, rice, pickles or *jareesh*. This is all wrapped up in the bread, swaddled in a piece of wax paper and eaten with gusto.

You can perhaps understand why, with all these goodies I am blithely devouring, I shall soon be a candidate for Miss Blimp of 1982. I must get out of here soon, but now I understand there is another religious holiday coming up and all the offices will be closed for a while. I begin to wonder if I shall ever see home again. If I had some mail it would help, but I feel very cut off from everyone and miss news of my older daughter, Trish. I know I didn't have to make this journey, so I have no one to blame, and quite frankly I would do it again in a minute. But now I am ready to bid everyone farewell and it just isn't all that easy to do. In a few days, God willing, Jewaher or Abduraman will bestir themselves on our behalf and exit visas will be forthcoming. Give my love to everyone.

Affectionately,

Babs

Dearest Aunt Helen,

More excitement to tell you about today! One day last week I walked in to the sitting room to find Jameil, one of my favourite people, gasping for breath and in obvious anguish. No one was paying any attention to her and her usually brown face was a peculiar ashen shade, her skin covered with perspiration. She bent over the burner on the floor, attempting to carry out her duties of preparing the coffee.

'Enti maritha?' I asked. What a silly question, of course she was sick! Why was no one concerned? They always became panicky when one of the family was ill or hurt. I found Nura and began the process, one-third Arabic, one-third English, and one-third gestures. What was wrong with Jameil and why wasn't anything being done about it? Nura explained that Jameil had been taken sick while scouring her bathroom and they would probably take her to a doctor later on if she didn't recover.

Returning to the sitting room I found Jameil worse rather than better, and motioned to her to show me what she had been doing. Grateful for my attention, she led me to her quarters and I found the strong bleach and scouring powder she had mixed in order to scrub the shower. Her breathing was coming in long, ragged gasps as she struggled to fill her constricting lungs with air. I felt a panic rising in myself at the thought of how I was to make everyone understand the urgency of getting her to a hospital at once. I raced back to the sitting room and tried to remain calm as I confronted Jewaher. It seemed like an eternity before she understood that I wanted a car and driver immediately to take Jameil to the hospital emergency ward. It must have seemed far longer to the frightened and agonised Jameil. Once Mustaffa was summoned, however, he grasped the situation quickly and dashed for the car. Jameil would not let go of my hand as we climbed inside; Nura ran after us with my veil.

At the hospital they were wonderful. Within minutes we

were in an examination room and a nurse was taking over. And blessed relief, everyone spoke English! In fact now the problem was the reverse, they did not speak Arabic and we could not make Jameil understand that she must remove her veils and clothing. She had taken off the veil for the nurse, but when the doctor arrived she quickly donned it and refused to 'come out'. We coaxed and cajoled, but she would have none of it. I tugged, she clutched. The veils were firmly in place. At last an overworked interpreter arrived. It took a lot more talking than you would expect under the circumstances, but at last either the severe pain or the words of the interpreter helped Jameil to realise she must remove the veils if she was to receive help. My heart ached for her as she sat there on the examining table, a mixture of pain and embarrassment. After a superficial examination, medication was given to ease the breathing and preparation was made for a more extensive inspection. Oh, no! If you think getting Jameil out of her veils was rough, just wait till we tried to get her out of her clothes! *No* way! Back came the harried interpreter, out went the doctor. The nurse and I stood there holding huge sheets while the interpreter explained that she would be securely covered by them. Jameil was not so easily assured. 'If she could be covered in those sheets, then why couldn't she just keep her clothes on?' That one stumped me, but fortunately it wasn't up to me to do the arguing. If it had, she would no doubt still be in her clothes, all *three* dresses and pantaloons as it turned out. Once again the wisdom and tact of the interpreter won out and she was finally ready for the doctor to examine her. She held on to me with a death grip but allowed him to check her thoroughly.

She had indeed inhaled a considerable amount of the toxic gases she had created when combining the cleaning agents. It was necessary to inject a medication into an artery. The doctor issued the order and we settled down to wait the very brief time it took for the medication to arrive.

Meanwhile, the doctor and nurse, whose name turned out to be Laural, regaled me with stories of the continuous difficulties they encountered in trying to minister to the Arabic women. The first problem was obviously that of trying to get them out from under their veils long enough to determine what was ailing them.

When the medicine arrived we were in for another ordeal. Jameil's skin texture was as tough as an elderly rhino's. She was also fat! Getting a needle into that artery was not an easy matter. The doctor shoved and poked, searched and shoved again. Jameil lay there stoically, only the tightening grip on my hand betrayed the increasing pain in her arm as the doctor shoved the needle around trying to locate the elusive artery. Time went by, the doctor shook his head. He gave up and called for a colleague. Poor Jameil was having a hard time holding her arm out there for them to jab. I marvelled at her bravery. After what seemed like hours, but was in reality twenty minutes, of this probing they found the artery and, with a sigh of relief from us all, injected the medication.

That was not the last of the ordeals for poor Jameil. Now the doctor would need X-rays of her chest to be sure there was no serious damage. I understood what the doctor had said, but of course she didn't. The moment he was gone she leapt up and reached for her clothing.

'Here we go again,' I thought.

Sure enough, as we tried to explain she must go down to X-ray in her sheets, she shook her head furiously and grabbed her clothes. With a helpless laugh, Laural called for the interpreter one more time. It took a great deal more explaining before Jameil would agree to get in the wheelchair dressed only in sheets and allow herself to be wheeled out into the hall and down to the X-ray lab.

Laural was wonderful, draping and wrapping her so not even a little toe poked out, and then swathing the finished product in her own veils for the journey through the hallways. They had explained that if she were to dress again for the trip, she would need to undress in the lab, where only booths with skimpy curtains were available. That alone would not have been enough; it was Laural's promise to keep her so well wrapped that no one could possibly see her which finally did the trick. Practising medicine here must be a true experience.

With Jameil in the hands of the technicians, Laural and I

struck up an animated personal conversation. Oh, Lordy, it was good to talk to someone in my own language with no need to use one-syllable words and the present tense, accompanied by wild gestures.

What was she doing here? How long had she been here? Where was she from? How did I get here? Where was I from? How long was I staying? What was my life like? How did I like it? We each had a hundred questions.

Laural was a Canadian, about forty years of age and one of the most excitingly beautiful women I have ever seen. Thick, wavy, toffee-coloured hair looked even paler against her deep sun-tan. She literally glowed with health and vitality. I found her interest in life, her energy and enthusiasm fascinating. She found my experiences interesting. Although she had been stationed here for over four years she had never been inside a Saudi home. Wouldn't I come to dinner and meet her room-mates? They'd all love to hear of my life over here. And I must bring my daughter, too. Would I come to dinner? Would a Muslim go to Mecca? If the family would allow it, we would be there. Laural promised to call and find out if we would be able to keep the date.

I could hardly wait to get home and find out. The thought of a full evening of conversation was overwhelming. Not until this opportunity presented itself did I realise how much I missed being able just to sit and gossip with friends.

I was in seventh heaven when Jewaher readily agreed. This time, since there were no men involved, there shouldn't be any problem. But knowing how often Lindy and I had been disappointed over something we wanted to do, knowing how often we were all ready only to find there were no drivers available, I knew I would be a nervous wreck until we were actually on our way.

The next day as we were sitting out on the swings sipping our minted tea, I thought I should mention I was expecting a call.

'A nurse from the hospital is going to call me in a day or two, I think.'

'She comes four o'clock,' said Fatima.

'What?' I glanced at my watch. It was four minutes past four.

'You mean she is here, somewhere?' I asked excitedly.

'Where "here"?' was Fatima's response.

'Here, here,' I shouted, jabbing my finger at the ground. 'Here in harem.'

Fatima looked disgusted, 'No here, in hospital.'

I was completely non-plussed, 'You said she comes at four, it now four.'

'Maybe four yesterday,' replied Fatima complacently.

'Do you mean tomorrow?' I asked.

'Maybe, or maybe nine o'clock.'

Oh God! I clutched my forehead in despair. How could I get this straightened out? This was typical of so many of my conversations. It had actually been a miracle that the lines were clear long enough for Laural to get through anyway. I felt very despondent for I was sure I would never be able to reach her. I eyed Gada chatting on the phone. Finally she hung up and reached for her phone book. This meant she was going to call someone else, but there would be a minute before she was ready. I lunged for the phone. 'Gotta make a call,' I spluttered.

Gada, having relinquished the phone, was charmingly helpful. She rang information and found the number of the hospital for me. I tracked Laural down through the help of a sweet lady at the hospital reception desk. Laural laughed as she explained her fruitless efforts to contact me, and we decided on that Friday evening for dinner at her home. I had completely forgotten that Friday was the night of Jewaher's feast for Prince Abdullah. As a result I missed Jewaher's big social event of my stay. It was unfortunate timing.

I thought Friday would never come, but at last it did. I spent all day reminding everyone we were going to need a car and driver at seven-thirty. Nervously I dressed and went outside to wait. I couldn't believe it! Promptly at seven-thirty there was Jewaher's Cadillac and her driver. Oh, bless her dear heart! I wanted to run back inside and hug her! But no time, we were off, as excited as Cinderella going to the ball.

When we arrived at the huge compound where the nurses

lived, Laural came down to the gate to lead us to her apartment. Easier than trying to give instructions. It was interesting that we would not have been allowed inside unless she had notified the guard that we were coming. Our names were on his list of expected visitors.

Hamdi helped us out and promised to return about eleven. Laural shares her apartment with two other nurses, one Australian, one British. They did not have a choice as to room-mates but found they all got along very well. The Australian girl has only been with them a few months, but Laural and Joan have been together for several years. They have recently made the difficult decision to sign another two-year contract. Although life is very frustrating for single women, they have been induced by a huge pay increase they simply felt they could not turn down.

Living accommodation is not one of their complaints. The apartment is lovely. Three roomy bedrooms upstairs, while downstairs there is a cute, very modern kitchen, dining area, large living room, attractive powder room, hallway and adequate closet space.

Every possible kind of recreational facility is provided for them; tennis courts, cinemas, bowling alleys, swimming pools, handball, baseball and basketball facilities, everything one could think of. The problem is not with their housing, and the working conditions are not all that bad, though like most jobs, it has its share of annoyances. No, the problem is that of being single in the Arab world. They cannot go out without a man; they cannot go to the hotels in town without a date. No legal liquor is available; there are no cocktail lounges; nightlife is non-existent, except what they create for themselves within the confines of the base. We talked and talked!

It was a marvellous evening. Laural was even more radiant in a hostess gown than in her uniform, and they had gone all out to make the evening special. We started with glasses of home-made sherry, which was delicious. Perhaps it would not have been so great had it not been so long since I had a whiff of the stuff.

With dinner we had a real celebration! An airline pilot had smuggled in a bottle of wine for Laural and I'm sure no wine could ever have been more enjoyed. The time really sped by and soon it was time for us to return to the harem, but not without assurances that should I still be here when the girls returned from a trip to Greece the following week, we would get together again. One of the pleasures of their contract is the fact that they are able to travel a great deal. Schedules are set to take advantage of it, and they have been all over the eastern world, to India and Egypt, as well as to Greece, Italy, Spain and more. High pay, reasonable working conditions, attractively furnished housing and travel opportunities lure foreign workers to this distant land.

It was interesting to view Saudi Arabia through the eyes of Laural and her room-mates. I think they were equally entertained to view it through ours. They had a million questions for Lindy, and I noticed that she did not recommend life as a Saudi wife. This is a departure indicative of her final rejection of her role. She is an extremely loyal person, and hitherto has staunchly maintained that the fault was mainly in her failure to adjust. Never was there the slightest criticism of her husband. Now she admitted to feeling both deserted and resentful of the unhappy, lonely life she was forced to live behind the wall while her husband went wherever he wished.

Laural commiserated, saying she had been engaged to a Saudi herself back home, which was why she had decided to apply for a position here to begin with. A little wiser than Lindy, apparently, she had wanted to see the world she would live in first-hand before making a final commitment. But once back home, her fiancé apparently became a different personality. He doffed his western behaviour and orientation as he doffed his western business suit. 'Arab men all seem to shed our western culture the moment they step off the plane and put on their Arabian robes. I found myself no longer a part, or seemingly not an important part, of his life. I broke the engagement after only a few months.'

The girls' stories of having to cope with the superstitions and religious restrictions of the people were fascinating. Medicine practised as it is in the western world is another new concept for the Saudis to come to terms with. Some simply will not go near the health clinics and hospitals the government has provided for all its citizens. Their faith is firmly planted with their M'Tawas, they are extremely sceptical of western doctors and their strange medical practices.

The M'Tawa is a sort of 'holy healer' rather like an Indian medicine man. Some of the practices, while unpleasant and drastic, do seem to work. One of the most ghastly, from my point of view, is based on the principle of acupuncture, only the *M'Tawa* applies the tip of a red-hot poker to certain points on the body to scare out the evil *jinn*. Most of the women I have seen bear scars the size of a man's thumbnail on their heads and necks to rid them of headaches.

My son-in-law was very ill when he was an infant and Jewaher called the M'Tawa. As a result he has a row of these round scars across his abdomen, both vertically and horizontally. The educated men of Jewaher's family were angry with her, and when my son-in-law grew up and became aware of western medical practice, he warned Jewaher that he never wanted to see evidence of a M'Tawa's ministrations on any of his younger brothers and sisters. Jewaher has obeyed these directives and none of the children have been so treated, but she herself, when western medicine fails, calls in the M'Tawa for help. Sometimes he is successful. As for my son-in-law, who knows whether or not he would have recovered without this dire treatment? Who knows what an American doctor might have done? Perhaps the M'Tawa saved his life; perhaps the pain and scars were needless.

Isn't medicine an interesting field? If the patient dies we know the treatment was unsuccessful, but if the patient recovers we never know for sure just who or what was responsible, and to what degree. I once knew a very fine surgeon who used to say, 'A little Christian Science never hurt anyone.'

As September disappears into the stuff of yesterdays, I note the coming of October with eyebrows high in surprise that I am still part of the Saudi scene. Talk about the man who came to dinner! I came for a month and am now beginning my fourth. Well, La Jolla is beautiful at this time of year and fortunately will still be beautiful when I get there, whenever that may be. Are you and Lil still taking your daily walk barefoot in the sand? You certainly couldn't walk barefoot on the sands around here! Everyone takes their shoes off at the door and there are always a pile of them outside Jewaher's sitting rooms. She wears her, though, I'm not sure why, but even Prince Abduraman removes his. I'm sure everyone wishes Jewaher would leave her clogs too, but I bet if she did they wouldn't be there when she went for them.

Give my best to all the 'Hags'. I must ask you to tell me someday how such a bunch of glamour gals ever came up with a name like that for your clique. Now over here there really are some old crones that would do justice to the name, if not the game.

Much love to you doll,

Babs

Highlights from the
Harem
October is here!

Dearest Aunt Joie,

I wonder where you are? Off on a jaunt somewhere, no doubt. Perhaps you and Madeline are taking in the theatre season in London again? Still, this time of year is so beautiful in Pennsylvania; perhaps you are enjoying a lovely Indian summer at home? The weather here is beginning to cool down a bit, and sitting outside in the late afternoon is quite pleasant in spite of the long skirts. I shall be happy to get back into short ones again, though, and also to become reacquainted with jeans and slacks for casual wear. Here, I always feel as if I am ready for the ball.

It is amazing to see the older Bedouin women wear as many as three dresses, one on top of the other, plus the full, loose pantaloons they have underneath, and all their veils. One would think they might just melt away on a hot day. I do not find that a goodly supply of clothing insulates and cools; I simply fry. In case you are thinking it is a difference in the material, they are wearing the same synthetics that we do now. Synthetics are really big here, but they also wear a lot of pure silk. I have been having my usual struggle to have a dress made; it is a lovely peach chiffon covered with small buds embroidered in gold.

I was so fond of this particular material Jewaher gave me that I did not want to let the Pakistani tailors ruin it, so they took me to a very special Egyptian woman who is supposed to do excellent work (she does a lot for Gada) but who is horrifyingly expensive. The woman took my measurements, I selected a picture from a magazine of a dress I would like to have, and she told me to return in one week for a fitting. Perhaps you can guess that over a month went by before I could prevail on any one to take me back for it, and when I finally managed to get there, she had lost my measurements, the picture of the dress, everything but the material itself. Fortunately she still had that. We started over again. It took quite a few weeks before I was able to return for the preliminary fitting; still more time has elapsed and I have not yet been able to have the final fitting. Hopefully, before I leave this dress will be finished!

These delays and procrastinations are often infuriating but generally just irritating. They will tell you, 'We are going at noon tomorrow,' so at noon you are all set to go and everyone is sitting around sipping tea. Suddenly four or five hours later, or maybe even three or four days later, someone will burst in shouting. 'Aren't you dressed? Everybody is waiting!'

At first I used to throw something on in a panic and dash out, full of secret anger that they had not had the courtesy to let us know of the change in plans, and stuttering out a public apology for being late. As this state of affairs continued, and I found this was the way of life, I decided I would just have to train them to be more considerate, or to organise better, or to stop saying they were going to do something they didn't intend to do, or something. I wasn't really sure just what they were doing, but I did know we never seemed to be ready at the right time. Either we were all dressed for an outing that mysteriously never materialised, or we'd give up and take a shower, a nap or something, when suddenly it would be time to go, and I was pretty tired of it. If they didn't tell me what was going on, they would just have to sit in the car and wait (all ten or twenty of 'em) while I showered and dressed. I *wouldn't* rush!

The first time I employed this conditioning technique I was inwardly scared to death they might go off without me and I'd miss out on the big event of the week. They didn't, but each time I had the same inward feeling of panic and, unfortunately, I didn't seem to be accomplishing anything. The problem seemed to be that they don't *mind* sitting packed in a car in 120° heat. They are all delighted to see me when I saunter out, my American innards boiling and bubbling from trying *not* to rush. After a while I gave up, and now I simply do my best to keep calm and accept the situation.

In my efforts to tell everyone about all the different sights and situations I am seeing or involved in, I wonder if I am giving an erroneous feeling of being always on the go. Lindy spends more and more of her time sleeping. When awake we play with the baby, play cards or sit and talk. For me the vast majority of hours in each day are spent merely sitting, quietly watching if something is going on, but more often than not, simply staring into space, lost in thought. The noise around us is always at a high level so it is not necessarily a tranquil experience. Jewaher screams at the servants and her children; the television blares so the listeners can hear it over Jewaher's tirade; three or four of the smaller children will be racing around the room with their toy cars, or fighting, or crying at the top of their lungs because they were just the loser in such a fight. Faisal will have his pocket radio going full-blast, and, miraculously, Gada will somehow be carrying on the inevitable telephone conversation amidst the din. While all this goes on, the incongruity of sitting there, sipping coffee, and then tea, and then another round of coffee, as if life were never-endingly tranquil and serene, seldom occurs to me. The lack of physical movement on the part of the older members of the family and their guests, coupled with the sipping of the drinks, gives an illusion of calm, and a frequent sense of overpowering boredom.

The highlight of the last couple of days was watching Jewaher have the hair removed from her arms. Incidentally, in case you are ever in an experimental mood and are feeling brave, I'll give you the recipe for the *halawa* they use. *Halawa* is candy – in fact, I guess it is just toffee, but they certainly put it to an unusual use, wouldn't you say?

3 cups water
3 cups sugar
lemon juice

Mix this until blended and turn onto a marble counter. Let it dry, peel it off and work it as you do toffee. When it's smooth and sticky, take about a tablespoonful and apply it to the area of skin you wish to depilate. Pull quickly. Do not smear the entire arm or leg at one time but work in small areas about two inches square.

Aunt Helen used to tell me about a substance her servant used when she lived in China, but I don't believe it was the same. I think it was a wax similar to that which can be purchased today in the States.

As I write this they have come to replenish the water supply in my refrigerator. Everyone drinks bottled water imported from France, and I cannot imagine the amount this huge establishment goes through in a day. No one is at all concerned with conserving it and water is used very freely. All the Saudi homes I have been in use this bottled water for drinking and cooking. For bathing and for household chores the water from the desalination plants is used. Again, the amount must be staggering, for the Saudi people are so clean. Clothes are spotless and baths are frequent. I'm sure no one limits themselves to one a day. Just imagine having to import all your drinking water and then failing to treat it as a scarce commodity!

It is strange to live in a country where, because of the great oil wealth, people have no sense of the value of things. Everything they need is there or can be purchased in an endless supply. Money itself is apparently unlimited. Jewaher carries with her a quilted purse which contains nothing but hundred-riyal notes. That is about $30 American. Each morning she has the servant open the safe and grabs a handful of these hundred-riyal notes to stuff in her bag. I don't know how much it is in total, but the handful is about two inches thick.

During the day Jewaher dispenses largesse to various family members, servants and merchants, sending her own personal servants back to refill the purse whenever large amounts have been used. One son asked for money to purchase some special *oudh* for a party he was giving; this took several purses full. Another needed additional funds to satisfy a large debt he had incurred on a recent trip. Fatima borrowed from her in order to buy a particularly expensive Paris gown she wanted for a special party. And throughout the day, whenever one of the younger children cries, she reaches into her purse and hands him one or two notes with which to buy candy. Can you believe handing one of your children $60 to run to the corner shop for candy? 'And keep the change, honey!' Naturally, these kids do a lot of unnecessary bellowing; it's good business.

All this casual dissemination of money gives one the illusion that it is some sort of 'play money'. I find myself wanting to stand in line for a handful of the stuff. But, I'm also becoming insensitive to the tremendous amount of cash flow that takes place each day in Jewaher's portion of the royal residence alone.

Incidentally, it might interest you to know that because Arabia's second language is English, all the money is printed with Arabic on one side and English on the other. Also, all the merchants speak at least some English, and quite a few speak it just as well as I do, being young men who were educated in the west. This has at least made shopping quite simple, once I get to the store!

There are supposed to be 'around' six million people in Saudi Arabia. The people are casual about numbers and written records vary, but anyway, the point I want to make is that, of this number, half a million women have managed to receive a formal education. The schools are, of course, unisex and are supervised by the *ulama* or religious leaders. It is expected that about forty thousand of these women will go on to receive college degrees within the next five years. It is unfortunate that, as yet, they are unable to use their education in any fields where they will come in contact with men. This means they are limited to education, nursing and welfare work.

The first welfare agency was started just twenty years ago by Princess Sara, the daughter of King Faisal. She had to promise, though, that it would be done very quietly and discreetly. It was intended mainly to improve the lot of Saudi women by providing adult literacy classes and hygiene clinics. In no way was it to conflict with the Islamic laws regarding the place of women. Some of these educated women are now campaigning to enter other career fields. Some have already done so, *sub rosa*.

This is another conflict that besets the culturally beleaguered country. As women become educated and join the workforce they can be of great value to their labour-impoverished nation, where even sensitive government positions must be filled by foreigners, but they also begin to demand new freedoms that conflict with Islamic teachings. The young men are still looking for traditional wives and will not consider an emancipated bride. A woman thus runs the very real risk of spinsterhood if she allows her education to lead her to a career. A few have determinedly made this choice, but the married state, be it happy or otherwise, is still the desire of the vast majority of Arabic women.

Gada's failure to marry is a great sorrow and concern to the entire family and the subject of much prayer. After all, according to the Koran, the only reason she was placed on this earth was to bring pleasure to a man. If she doesn't fulfil this role there doesn't seem to be any reason or purpose to her very existence. She doesn't even have career aspirations that might offer some compensation. One can't help but speculate as to how it will all turn out . . . what life will be like for the Saudi people five years from now. There is much to be admired here that could be lost. Change is inevitable, but their family ways and traditions seem so right for them that it will indeed be sad if they are destroyed at the expense of entering the twentieth century.

Speaking of family, give my love to Bill, Joanne, and their families. I'm so looking forward to seeing them all again.

Much love dear one.

Babs

My dear Bob,

Hey, is anybody out there? Did you ever have the feeling you might be the last American (or in your case, Canadian) on the planet? It has been many days since my last contact with reality and I am beginning to wonder. How do the Saudi and American businessmen carry on their affairs? By telex and telephone, I suppose. I have managed to grab the phone a few times and rather guiltily tried to put through a call to Trish but I've never been able to get a free line to the States. In my anxiety to get out of here, and to force them to stop procrastinating, I'm afraid I am not as pleasant as I could be under all circumstances. Life here is beginning to take its toll of my nerves.

I have had several lovely experiences lately, though, and must share them with you.

Last week I was telling one of the uncles how interested I am in the history and development of the country and how I wished it were possible to see some of it the way it used to be. Apparently he relayed this to the girls or Jewaher, for a few days later they bundled us into the car with an air of suppressed excitement and secrecy. We drove out into the desert for about an hour, and then suddenly came upon an oasis with an old Bedouin ruin. The buildings were built of a type of sand brick and grass that blended so well into the surrounding dunes that we were upon them before I realised they were there.

We arrived at sunset, and it was a beautiful sight. The crumbling walls were turned a pink-gold hue by the sinking sun, and purple shadows lay along the twisting, turning paths that ran in every direction. The old walls with their key-hole windows were etched against the rose-coloured sky as it rapidly darkened to mauve. Originally the buildings stood three stories high and were all contained inside a high wall with look-out towers, now broken down for the most part, but here and there, like tired but courageous old men, standing tall and weary-looking, giving evidence of past strengths.

Staircases were narrow, dark and spiral, carved from the soil or built with the bricks, but crumbling and treacherous either way. I thought of how they would not have been all that much safer or easier to tread in their original state, being steep, twisting and narrow, with no evidence of past handrails that I could see. Doors were rough – vertical boards held by wooden cross-bars secured with large studded nails. They were very low and I was forced to stoop almost double to enter the dark little rooms that chased each other around and up and down through the maze.

Lindy and I were in seventh heaven and the girls were delighted at our obvious enjoyment of the lovely spot. It was the desert of Omar Khayyam and the Sheik of Araby all rolled into one. If you ever have an opportunity to visit a desert ruin, be sure to do so by sunset; it was so gloriously beautiful!

The family were all so pleased with our joy over that outing, they planned another surprise for us, and a few days later we set out again. This time the trip was twice as long and the ruins were twice as large. Jewaher told me they had been there for about one hundred and fifty years. I couldn't get over them. They were just as left; no one had been there to disturb them. In the States not a shred of evidence would remain that anyone had ever inhabited something that long ago. Vandals, historians and ordinary tourists would long since have stripped the place bare.

Here there are no tourists and the historians have not yet realised what they have, or have been too busy with other such sights to bother with this one. The people themselves see nothing unusual in them, and are lacking in curiosity about a way of life they have only recently left behind.

Here, as I clambered, with long skirts hiked up and sweat streaming down my face, over, under and into every corner, I found old camel saddles, woven baskets so rotted away that they fell from their wooden pegs at my touch, the remains of clothing and cooking implements. Cupboard doors were intricately carved and the paint was still visible in the designs. Huge iron locks held them in place. Lindy, once an archaeology major, was simply thrilled, I haven't seen her so happy since my arrival.

After the desecrated and despoiled ruins of our own country and Europe, always crowded with tourists, this untouched spot was almost too much to comprehend. The girls had sat patiently in the car throughout our explorations, and so we had wandered, totally alone except for the driver, over the old paths and through time-worn buildings, under ageing palm trees. We gazed down at the remains of the huge old wells, and stood for a few reverential moments in the mosque, which had somehow, miraculously, withstood the ravages of the years, looking as it must have done one hundred and fifty years ago when men knelt on its dirt floor to render their prayers to Allah.

As if this experience weren't enough. there was more in store for us. On the way home we passed through an old but inhabited village! Here the people were almost as intrigued by us as we were by them. I'm sure some of them had never seen an unveiled American woman before! This time I had left my veil at home, for they had told me we were just riding out into the desert and would see no one. The girls had done the same. It was a great relief to be without them in the desert heat, but here we were causing a considerable furore. They kept their own women inside (we saw a few peering out of windows behind their own discreet veils) but the men and children followed us everywhere. They posed eagerly for pictures and begged us to enter their homes, more accurately described as hovels, to have tea.

We accepted one such invitation and entered through a metal door painted and decorated with turquoise blue. The floors were of dirt and the ceilings so low that when I stood erect they were but inches from the top of my head. It was very dark, the light entering through tiny slits in the wall, and the rooms were like rabbit warrens – many tiny little cubicles connected by narrow, low passageways with a variety of nooks and crannies.

Clothing and food hung intermingled from wooden hooks driven into the ceilings. A small hole in the floor connecting, I suppose, to some sort of drainage, and a cauldron of water in one cubicle about four feet high, was the bathroom. Ledges cut into the walls with woven mats in another area appeared to be the sleeping quarters.

The water for tea and coffee was heated in a pot slung on a hook over a fire pit in the centre of the floor in one small room. To say the accommodations were primitive is a quaint understatement, but the courtly charm and graciousness of the old gentleman belied the humble surroundings. King Khalid in his palace could not have been a prouder host.

When we left the village, after many farewells in the flowery formality of the Arab world, everyone assured me that these people were not poor, but in fact are quite well off, receiving as they do their share of the oil moneys and being eligible for all the free necessities provided by the government. Indeed they had several big, late-model cars and a variety of trucks in the alleys, and the few women I managed to catch a glimpse of were wearing enough gold bracelets on their arms to buy Fort Knox. For reasons of their own, the people like their homes as they are and choose to remain there. It was fascinating.

For contrast, last night I was the dinner guest of Prince Saleh and his American wife. They are a fine example of how the western-educated members of the royal family are arranging and living their lives. His other brother, Prince Abduraman, Lindy's father-in-law, was educated in the ways of the desert. He is happiest when out at the ranch, and has no interest in building a fortune. He leaves the running of the family business to his partner. On the other hand, Prince Saleh, twelve years younger, was sent to Harvard to further his education. He has a master's degree in business, and married an attractive American woman. As a busy, productive businessman he travels extensively, but considers Saudi Arabia his home. His residence is large, luxurious, and filled with paintings and *objets d'art* he collects as investments. Currently he is building a new home in Paris which he says will complete his 'set' of six.

The house is equipped with riding stable, tennis court, bowling alley, indoor and outdoor pools, squash court, billiard room and large library. By anybody's standards the couple live in princely style. The American princess has trained her servants well and the household runs smoothly. The cuisine is excellent. The home looks much as you would find in upper strata America, but if male friends of Saleh were to arrive, his wife and I would have to retire to her quarters and dine alone. Westernisation is not total.

In the course of the evening's conversation, Saleh made several points that I have heard many times from young Arabs in the States, and from the various male relatives I have talked to over here. The Saudis fully expect that the rest of the world will have found another source or supply of energy within the next five years. That gives them just five years to make Saudi Arabia self-sufficient in terms of its own educated work force and its own industries. They want to be ready at the end of that time to take their place as an independent country amid the first world nations. Ten years ago they were excited at the prospect of joining the nations of the free world against the communist bloc. Now they feel a sense of betrayal and there is talk that, in view of United States' attitudes, perhaps they should look elsewhere for their alliances.

Saudia is currently dependent on the west for its cash flow, its technological development, its trained scientists, engineers and industrialists of every kind. The west needs their oil. It is a symbiotic relationship. Saleh and other wealthy Saudis are busy building their own fortunes both in and out of Saudi Arabia, ensuring the continuance of their own personal wealth to the best of their ability. They are also deeply committed to the development of their own country and feel a concern and resentment toward the United States for its manner of total self-interest. They feel we do not appreciate what they have done for us, and that we exploit them daily for our own ends. Arabia has held oil prices down at a sacrifice of almost $100,000,000 per day, and at the request of the United States government, the daily output of oil has been increased even though to do so depletes the country's only natural resource.

They feel they have done their best to be a loyal, helpful ally in the present energy crisis. They have looked to us as a strong ally against the communist threat and now wonder how dependable we will be if we have no further need of their oil.

Saleh is very bitter about the way Reagan and congress handled the AWACS situation. He feels, along with many others, that America humiliated them before the entire world, when as friends and close allies they asked for the AWACS as a means of defending their borders and America replied with long congressional debates. It brought home the words of the Koran sharply:

'Believers, take neither Jews nor Christians for your friends. They are friends with one another. Whoever of you seeks their friendship shall become one of their number. Allah does not guide the wrongdoers.'

'The Jews control Washington,' Saleh said with great bitterness. 'Your government has engaged in a policy of duplicity since the days of Truman.'

In 1945 Ibn Saud met President Roosevelt and received a promise from him that the problem of the Jewish settlement in Palestine would be settled satisfactorily. Then Truman became president and broke the promise, throwing strong support to the cause of Israel. It was to this that Saleh referred in his conversation with me.

'We cannot depend on U.S. promises; they change with the coming of each new administration. All they want from us is our oil!'

I had no words to refute this, and knowing the attitudes of many of my countrymen toward the Arab people, I was reminded again of words in the Koran, and of how they live meaningfully in today's world, just as they did in the days of Mohammed:

'Believers, do not make friends with any men other than your own people. They will spare no pains to corrupt you. They desire nothing but your ruin. Their hatred is clear from what they say, but more violent is the hatred which their breasts conceal.'

In fact as I think of this, it is amazing to me that we were ever able to convince the Saudi rulers to let us share in the wealth of their land, or to form an alliance with us, when you consider how deeply they believe in and follow the words handed down to them by their Prophet.

It was a lovely evening, one of the pleasantest of my stay, and also one of the most informative. America would do well to listen to the articulate young men of Arabia who are currently acquiring their education in our schools. They go home to help build their country in spite of their profligate ways while away from home. They are intelligent, emotional and extremely bitter. Their thoughts and feelings will have great bearing on Saudi-American relationships to come.

On the personal side, the family seems to have agreed that both Lindy and I may return home and that Tarek may go with us, yet nothing is done. Constant evasions, delays and excuses. Now they say we cannot go until appropriate servants have been found to accompany the little prince, ones who have been satisfactorily trained and are willing to go to America. Since I have been approached four or five times by servants begging to be taken to 'Amereka' when I go, I can't see why they are having so much trouble.

Since Abdul Raman also agreed that Lindy should return, we have seen and heard nothing of him. We now do not have even his occasional appearances to help straighten out confused situations caused by language difficulties. I am becoming increasingly apprehensive; no one seems concerned with *my* need to return to my own country either. Saleh said he would talk with his brother, but he has made promises to do things in the past and forgotten. After all, as the head of a huge, multi-faceted business he has much else on his mind.

If only there were something I could do. We can't walk out across the desert, and there seems to be no other way. I have tried to be somewhat casual about my concern in my letters to my family, but I confess to you a real sense of increasing panic.

Ah, but what an experience! I know I wouldn't have missed it for anything I can think of at present. If only my daughter's unhappiness were not a part of it.

Love to you,

Babs

My darling daughter,

I cannot believe what is happening! I am going home at last, but my heart is breaking. Lindy is not going with me! Oh, they say she is, they say she will follow soon . . . soon. But after what we have gone through, how can we believe them? How can I go away and leave her here alone? We are sure they will just continue to delay and make excuses, keeping her here indefinitely, and there isn't a thing I can do. It is this feeling of total helplessness that is so difficult for outsiders to bear. We are no longer masters of our own fate.

We are sure they think that if I leave, Lindy will adjust and they will not lose their only grandchild. Actually, I can honestly say I bear no responsibility for Lindy's decision. Opposed, as you know, to the marriage to begin with, once it took place I was as dedicated to its success as anyone, and never would I try to undermine it. However, I can understand their thinking. Jewaher and Abduraman are naive and simplistic in many ways, and just cannot understand why either Lindy or myself need more from life than the ease, comfort and security of a harem.

Once they made the decision that I must go, the obstacles to my departure blew away like sand in a windstorm. After not a word but excuses for all these weeks, suddenly yesterday morning, without a word of warning, I was awakened at the unheard-of hour of nine o'clock. We had all gone to bed about 4:30 a.m., so no one was up when my maid dashed in to tell me to hurry and dress because the driver was waiting outside in the car to take me to the photographer for my visa pictures.

I'll tell you, I thought I was dreaming. Could it really be happening after all this time? I thought Saleh must have kept his promise to speak to Abduraman.

When everyone finally sauntered out I discovered there was much excitement. I was told that I now have five days to leave the country or my visa will no longer be valid. I also learned that Lindy would not be going with me. 'Her papers are not ready,' they said. Gada also stated that if I remain in the country after my five days are up, the authorities will put me in prison. I imagine that is possibly what could happen if the prince withdrew his protection, as I would then be here illegally. Then came the news that because this is the time of the Hadj (religious journeys to Mecca), every available flight out is booked solid with a long waiting list. But everyone assured me 'not to worry'.

'There will always be a seat for the grandmother of a prince,' they said, 'we will simply have someone removed.'

Much as I want to go, I don't want to go without Lindy, and the thought of doing so at the expense of someone else also upsets me. Now that I am about to leave, I find myself with mixed emotions (apart from my concern about Lindy). I have seen and learned so much during my stay and have developed a real affection for the people. As my understanding of their ways and their beliefs grew, my tolerance also grew. I no longer wish to change them, to mould them into carbon copies of myself and my friends. As they have said so many times, they have their ways, and their ways are to be accepted and appreciated for themselves.

I love them for their fierce and loyal pride in their own country and all things Arabic. I admire them for their marvellous feeling of family unity. Family not only in the consanguineous sense, but also in the belief that their country is composed of one large family, the Sauds, each with his or her own duty and responsibility to that country, and each with knowledge of the support and protection that will always be available. It is this feeling of 'family solidarity', the feeling of closeness to their king, that makes one feel revolution is a remote possibility in this country.

Within the precepts of the Koran, the Muslim is a man of honour, with a strict code by which he lives. If to us his ways seem dishonourable at times, it is because we fail to understand there is no injunction against such actions or statements in the Koran. For Muslims, the Koran is the infallible word of God. According to N. J. Dawood, an Iraqi writer and translator, 'It is a literary masterpiece of surpassing excellence.' Mohammed Marmaduke Pickthall seems closer to the emotion with which the Muslim views his holy book when he calls it 'The glorious Koran, that inimitable symphony, the very sound of which moves men to tears and ecstasy.'

When read through the eyes of an infidel such as myself, it seems drearily repetitious, and the reference to slaves and *jinni* seem archaic for a daily creed, but there are times when it is ageless and uncannily atune to the happenings of today. As a literary masterpiece, however, I must agree with H. G. Wells, who said, 'Regarded as literature or philosophy the Koran is certainly unworthy of its alleged Divine authorship.' I can only assume it loses a great deal in translation.

Be that as it may, you cannot begin to know or understand an Arab without first knowing the Koran, and realising what it is that rules his life, his political as well as his personal and business life. So one of the big problems for the Saudis, as I see it, is that they always look to the past for today's answers. Answers are there, but they are based on values, beliefs, and cultural patterns that are almost 1400 years old.

Another problem is the very real identity crisis that faces each of the royal family in the teenage years. By training and upbringing they are taught to believe in their own importance, then suddenly they discover they are thought to be somehow inferior by much of the rest of the world. People are actually looking down at *them*, princes of the royal blood! Think what this must do to them psychologically! In America we make a fuss about the great stress of adolescence alone, which is far less than this additional terrible blow to the ego. They envy and imitate us, and is it any wonder they hate us? We are so sure of our own superiority, so smug in our knowledge that we are the greatest nation on earth, and, as individuals, so impressed with our own importance as Americans.

As they struggle to emerge from obscurity and ignorance are we genuinely trying to help them make the difficult adjustment, or are we sneering at their bewilderment and nescience? We shake our heads in disgust (tinged on occasion with more than a little envy, I suspect) at the conspicuous consumption and profligate tastes of the Arabs. How soon we forget the peccadillos of our own idle rich, which, when investigated, sometimes uncover scandals of lesbianism, sadism, murder, child neglect, drug abuse, adultery and degeneracy that would make Nero weep with envy. The debauched, surfeited behaviour of the bored 'upper-class' of two continents at the turn of the century showed every excess and more of which we find the Arabs guilty. The avariciously acquisitive displays of poor taste that resulted in such overstuffed places as the Hurst palace, the Breakers, the Vanderbilt Mansion on Fifth Avenue, were the concupiscent product of *nouveau riche* and old money alike before the days of income tax. Sudden wealth always brings excesses and the Saudis are no more immune to it than anyone else.

After all, a scanty forty-eight years ago oil to an Arabian was something that came from an olive tree. You cooked with it and lit your lamp with it. Now they produce thirty per cent of the world supply. They have a surplus of around $150,000,000 every day after the basic needs for the people are taken care of. I wish I had such a problem with excess money, but I can understand their difficulty even though it doesn't move me to tears! They must modernize their country in keeping with religious restrictions, and must invest wisely so that when the west no longer needs their oil they will be self-sufficient. They are conservative in their financial policies, as in everything else. They invest in desalination plants, automobiles, electronics and hotels. Public money is invested in American companies to amounts somewhere close to twenty billion dollars. Ten per cent of their surplus is given away to other Arab countries in keeping with the injunction in the Koran to give alms.

The Saudi people are able to petition the government for loans to begin businesses or build houses or finance a wedding. Much of the loan need not be repaid. They are building their armed forces but must look to us for help in case of attack for their population is so small it is impossible to have a large army. At present the armed forces total less than sixty thousand. The air force is mostly comprised of Saudi family princes who have been trained in Britain and America. The whole subject of defence is naturally a big concern and herein lies the cause of much current resentment and distrust of the United States. They can't possibly protect their oil or their country against modern attack, but as allies of the United States they expected our full support. Now they see us as strongly supporting Israel and only interested in their oil. How much help can they realistically expect from us? Perhaps the U.S.S.R. would be a more reliable ally? In spite of a tradition of strong anti-communist feelings, they are having second thoughts, or at least some of them are.

From the United States, far more than our dollars, they want technological training and a pledge of support for their national security. They also want a solution to the Palestinian problem. Upset by the Camp David Accord, Crown Prince Fahd has devised a plan which is very popular here. It has done much to keep the Saudi heads high, to think that their country may come up with a solution for the rest of the world. It calls for a UN trusteeship over Gaza and the West Bank until an independent Palestinian state can take over. It doesn't say so explicitly, but it implies recognition of Israel. This will probably not be good enough for the Israelis but is an amazing breakthrough for an Arab country and is evidence of the sincere Saudi desire for a peaceful settlement. Unfortunately I'm sure the Israelis will never buy the idea that they give up all land gained after 1967.

I leave it to wiser heads than mine to determine where the United States' backing should be, but I sometimes wonder where those wiser heads are.

One thing I do know is that the Koran puts a curse on usury and blesses those who give alms, have faith in Allah and say their prayers. Good Muslims will be rewarded richly, and there is no doubt in the minds of these religious people that the oil so desired by the world was put in the Middle East by Allah. As far as they are concerned, Arabia is wealthy today because they have been devout believers in the Faith, not because America developed their oil reserves. What they must do now is find a way to retain their Islamic cultural values while developing their nation and educating their people. No easy task.

It is also no easy task for me to realise that after all this time I am about to 'fold my tent' and leave this exotic land. Sometime within the next three days I will no doubt hear shouts of, 'Yella, yella' (Let's go!) and there will be the car and driver waiting to take me to the airport. That is when I shall begin to pack, for you see, I have learned the Saudi way of travel.

I know you will join me in prayers for your sister's welfare. We send our love to you as always.

Last lines from the harem, darling,

Mom

Dear Ruth and Andy,

My fantastic journey into another world has ended and I am embarked on a new adventure, travelling solo through Egypt, Greece, Italy and Spain as I slowly wend my way homeward.

I plan to arrive in New York around the end of November. If I make it by Thanksgiving, dear cousins, I would love to invite myself to spend it with you and your family at Collings Lake. Then I shall be on my way to Reading to visit my Aunt Joie for a couple of weeks before I head for California. I'll call you from Madrid to see if it's convenient and let you know just when to expect me.

Cairo is exciting, but due to the terrible murder of Anwar Sadat on October 7, the country is in official mourning and many places are closed. Armed guards are everywhere and each time I enter my hotel they search my purse and always laugh at how small it is. I'm obviously not able to hide a grenade or gun or something in it!

I was surprised at the reaction of the Egyptians to my expressions of regret. The people here are not the least unhappy to see the end of Sadat; they just regret the manner in which the change came about. They feel he was a personal glory-seeker, and not really interested in the welfare of Egypt. As for Mubarak, they take a 'wait and see' attitude. The people I have talked with – businessmen, housewives, clerks, taxi drivers and teachers – do not see peace as a preliminary to economic improvement. Certainly the poverty here is overwhelming and the dirt of the ages is everywhere. It is very different from Arabia, as are the people.

I find there is little love lost between the Arabians and the Egyptians. This does not surprise me, for Egyptians in Saudia were there as servants and labourers for the most part, and they resent the sudden wealth of their brother Muslims. Another thing that totally surprised me in Cairo is the large number of Jews who live here. I know of none in Saudi; I don't believe they are allowed in the country. Here I have been stopped on the street several times by frightened Jews who are trying to get out of the country and are unable to get a seat on the overcrowded planes and trains. They are terrified of reprisals if it is found that Israel was behind the assassination, though presently the government is constantly assuring us via all the media that it was not the work of the Israelis.

My last days in the harem were typical of my entire existence there. Nothing at all happened for several days and I began to feel sure I would not be leaving. My requests for a driver to gather up various objects, such as film from the photographer, my dress from the Egyptian dressmaker and so on, all went unnoticed. Then, suddenly, on the morning of my last day, everything was rounded up. My dress from the dressmaker didn't fit and the jacket hadn't been made, but it was too late now.

I discovered that in the dead of night Jewaher had departed for Mecca, taking Nura and Fatima with her, leaving the imperious and increasingly unfriendly Gada in charge. I will not be able to say goodbye and thank her for her hospitality. She, in turn, is relieved of the need to face me or go through any ritualistic goodbyes or exchange any parting gifts. I am sorry our relationship is ending like this. Again I suffer the confusion of trying to understand the Arabic mind. Am I being grandly snubbed? Openly insulted? Or does she wish to escape the need to explain the unpleasant fact that they are not honouring their agreement to let Lindy and the baby go with me? I will probably never know, but based on their general inclination simply to ignore unpleasantness, I tend to accept the latter idea.

Gada seemed highly relieved to be rid of me, and hustled me to the airport at two-thirty in the afternoon for a flight that I found was due to take off at five-thirty and actually did at eight-thirty. It was a long and tiring afternoon. I had left a stoically smiling Lindy at the gate. Now my days as a pseudo-Arabian princess are over, I think of the memories I take away with me. There are so many. Perhaps one day I shall write them all down.

Standing out strongly is the painful struggle of the worried older generation to preserve tradition and religious tenets, and the many members of the younger generation struggling for freedom to follow forbidden western ways. There is the feeling that growing resistance to, and resentment of, western values among much of the population accompanies a tightening of the ways of Islam. While there I met two young women who had been educated in London and were very modern in their thinking at one time. They had returned with vehemence to their traditional role as Saudi women, extolling its virtues to me, Lindy, Gada, Fatima, Nura and the rest at great length. They feel our ways are complex, vice-ridden and totally lacking in the love, warmth and security for women that is so much a part of Saudi life.

I recall with affection the multi-faceted personalities of the family: barbaric, naive, sweet, thoughtless, self-centred, generous, tempestuous, erratic, emotional, sentimental, loyal and full of charm. The women were dignified one moment, hoydens or harridans the next. The men were courteous, intelligent, kind, and to my western mind, completely overbearing and incredibly chauvinistic.

I recall the struggle I had to collect reliable data on anything. I have read vastly disparate accounts of how many people make up the royal family – from 2,000 to 5,000. Now that's a 3,000 differential, which is no mean margin of error, but I'll settle for the fact that there are quite a few of them! And then the population. Again I've read statistics ranging from five million to eight million. That's pretty casual accounting. I'm settling on about six.

I love the strength and confidence they draw from their religion, their joy in their children and their pride in their country.

I'm impressed that they are one of the world's leading foreign aid donors.

I hate their proclivity for lying about things, and with such equanimity, too!

I hate their lack of sensitivity to my need for privacy while protecting their own so assiduously.

And oh, how I detest their constantly casual approach to time!

I have a very strong desire to warn people to become very well informed on the people of Saudi Arabia, their culture, their religion and their beliefs, for they control a large portion of the world's finances and a large portion of a needed natural resource. Between the two they could make it a very different world for us if they so desire.

But my favourite memory will always be that of sitting in the courtyard with the family in the evening, the rich gowns and veils of the women contrasting sharply with the austere white *thopes* of the men. I can see so vividly the huge Arabian carpets spread out under the evening sky, the tops of date palms etched against the sunset's deepening glow beyond the harem wall. As the servants circle softly to refill our tiny cups yet again, the long-drawn call of the muezzins floats out over the city, calling the faithful to prayer. Jewaher gestures for her prayer rug and begins her evening ablutions, tended by a servant whose many gold bracelets flash in the moonlight. The air is warm and dry, scented with a mixture of *oudh* and many fragrances worn by the women. Soon the sky will darken to deep blue velvet spangled with stars, and a crescent moon will lend its touch of delicate silver beauty to the scene. It is truly the land of Scheherazade and I am content. It is a time of peace and reflection, a time for self-renewal.

I take with me a new-found patience, and a new understanding of the ways of others. I take most of all the memory of an extraordinary time in the life of this independent American woman. But I leave my heart behind with Lindy.

Fondly

Babs

EPILOGUE

King Fahd now sits on the throne of Saudi Arabia. As I had expected, his plan for a peaceful solution to the Palestinian problem was not accepted. Saudi-American relations are continuing to deteriorate. Lack of understanding between cultures continues.

For us, however, the story has a happy ending. My daughter, her little son, and one servant arrived back in the United States in January of 1982, three months after my departure from Saudi Arabia.

the family had indeed continued to practise a series of delaying tactics; no servant available, no exit visa, no passport for the baby, official offices closed, no papers for the servant once one was found, applications lapsed, holidays again, and so on.

Then one day Abdul Raman came home. After a heated argument with his father, he took matters into his own hands, spiriting them out, over the wall, to a waiting truck in the middle of the night. Officials were apparently bribed to overlook the absence of necessary papers, and Lindy was homeward bound.

She now resides in a pleasant apartment with my grandson and attends classes regularly to prepare herself for the career she needs to support herself and her child. The servant is gone and most of her jewels have been sold. Prince Abdul Raman sends money sporadically when he can, or when he remembers (the Saudi time concept again), but one cannot rely on it and it is just enough to cover daily living expenses. She has no furniture or home of her own. There is no glamorously large settlement. The family contributes nothing and the welfare of their grandson, the little prince, is apparently of no further interest to them.

People ask why Lindy does not sue for divorce and a large alimony or at least a permanent home for the baby and a guarantee as to his education. She is grateful for what Abdul Raman feels inclined to send her, for he does not need to send anything. There is no law court in America that can force a Saudi in Saudi Arabia to support a wife or an ex-wife and children in America if he doesn't wish to do so. It is to Abdul Raman's credit that he recognises any obligation at all, and we are eternally grateful that he defied his parents to help Lindy escape. For an Arabian son, that was no small thing!